Praise for *We*

"We, at Campbell Soup Company, have worked hard to achieve world-class levels of employee engagement, which in turn has driven success in all areas of the company. Karsan and Kruse offer compelling research and detailed advice that will enable leaders at all levels in an organization to step-up the emotional commitment they need from their team members to materially improve performance."

—DOUGLAS CONANT, CEO, CAMPBELL SOUP COMPANY

"If you think smoking kills, then you should know that having a bad job is just as lethal (literally) to both the employee and the company. What Rudy and Kevin understand is that both the employee and their leadership have dual roles in fixing this toxic situation—and they outline in detail the three drivers needed to create an engaged workplace, based on their experience and research from over 10 million people."

—VERNE HARNISH, CEO, GAZELLES INC.
AND AUTHOR OF *THE ROCKEFELLER HABITS*

"Karsan and Kruse show the power of having engaged employees for business success and provide practical guidance for how to achieve it."

—PETER CAPPELLI, PhD, THE WHARTON SCHOOL
AND AUTHOR OF *THE INDIA WAY*

"In my years as a business journalist I've interviewed, spent time with, and learned from hundreds of executives. Rudy Karsan's insights into career growth, employee engagement, and leadership have stood out. This book is a must read."

—ALI VELSHI, CNN ANCHOR AND CHIEF BUSINESS CORRESPONDENT

"The importance of engagement in your work cannot be overstated. Whether you're looking to make engagement a reality for yourself or your company, *We* provides the roadmap that will get you there."

—TRAVIS BRADBERRY, COAUTHOR OF THE BEST SELLER
EMOTIONAL INTELLIGENCE 2.0

"During these challenging times, Karsan and Kruse remind us that successful businesses are built by dedicated workers. *We: How to Increase Performance and Profits through Full Engagement* should be read by everyone interested in building high-performing teams."

—CONGRESSMAN PATRICK MURPHY, AUTHOR TAKING THE HILL

"For anyone who has not yet identified their dream job, Karsan and Kruse offer a framework built around passion, purpose, and pay that can guide you to career choices that will lead to full engagement."

—GAVIN KERR, PRESIDENT AND CEO, INGLIS FOUNDATION

"There are no more safe jobs—or safe industries! Security comes from the ability to reinvent your career at any time. With its deep insights and provocative questions, this book is an invaluable resource that will help you move into an exciting and engaging career."

—PAMELA MITCHELL, AUTHOR OF THE 10
LAWS OF CAREER REINVENTION

WE

WE

HOW TO INCREASE PERFORMANCE AND PROFITS THROUGH FULL ENGAGEMENT

RUDY KARSAN

KEVIN KRUSE

WILEY

John Wiley & Sons, Inc.

For general information on our other products and services or for technical support, please contact our Customer Care Department within the United States at (800) 762-2974, outside the United States at (317) 572-3993 or fax (317) 572-4002.

Wiley also publishes its books in a variety of electronic formats. Some content that appears in print may not be available in electronic books. For more information about Wiley products, visit our web site at www.wiley.com.

Illustrations by Deb Lee Toth.

Library of Congress Cataloging-in-Publication Data:

ISBN 978-0-470-76743-6 (cloth)

ISBN 978-1-118-01316-8 (ebk)

ISBN 978-1-118-01317-5 (ebk)

ISBN 978-1-118-01318-2 (ebk)

Printed in the United States of America

10 9 8 7 6 5 4 3 2 1

To my grandparents for their teachings, their sense of adventure, and most importantly, their unconditional love.

—RK

To my mother, who through her own dreams inspired me to write.

—KK

Contents

Foreword

In my book, *Delivering Happiness: A Path to Profits, Passion, and Purpose* (Business Plus, 2010), I write about how the number-one priority for us at Zappos is company culture. We believe that if we get the culture right, most of the other stuff, such as delivering great customer service or building a long-term enduring brand and business, will happen naturally on its own.

For us, it all starts with the hiring process. We do two sets of interviews. The first set is done by the hiring manager and his or her team, and is pretty typical, where we look for fit within the team, relevant experience, technical ability, and so on. Then, our HR department does a second set of interviews, looking purely for culture fit. Candidates have to pass both sets of interviews in order to be hired. Because of this, we've passed on a lot of very smart, talented people that we know could make an immediate impact on our top or bottom line; if they're not a culture fit, we won't hire them. Our ultimate goal is to create a culture of happy, engaged, and productive employees.

In *We: How to Increase Performance and Profits Through Full Engagement*, Rudy Karsan and Kevin Kruse offer their insights drawn from their own experiences as well as from studying over 10 million employees around the world. They offer self-assessments and practical advice, which are designed to help you maximize your happiness at work. Managers can learn how to create an environment that fosters growth, recognition, and trust.

Happy, engaged, and productive employees lead to happy and repeat customers. This book can be an important step to help all of us maximize happiness and engagement at work.

—Tony Hsieh, #1 *New York Times* best-selling author
of *Delivering Happiness* and CEO of Zappos.com, Inc.

Introduction

We'd love to get to know you better. Where do you work?

What does your employer do?

No, really, we want you to answer that specific question—*out loud*. It's a little exercise (we know it's dangerously early in a book to be making you work). Just describe out loud—in a sentence or two—what your organization does.

Did you do it?

Okay, here's the reveal. Did you say "we" or "they" when you described what your employer does? Did you say something like "*We* produce widgets for the automotive industry" or "*They* produce widgets for the automotive industry"?

That's what we call the "We Test."

You can tell a lot about an organization's culture and whether workers are fully engaged in their jobs by how often they use the word *we* as opposed to *they*, *our*, or even *I*.

- Do you say, "I'm the assistant manager on *Jane's* team" or "I am the manager for *our* team?"

- Do you say, "*I* had the best quarter so far; sales were up 20 percent" or "*Our team* had the best quarter so far; sales were up 20 percent"?

You can even hear the difference when people complain about their jobs.

- A disengaged customer service rep might say, "Work sucks. *They* haven't filled the open positions yet so I'm handling way too many calls."
- A fully engaged customer service rep might comment, "Work sucks lately. *Our* recruiting efforts haven't been very effective so *we're* handling more than calls than normal."

The premise of this book is simple but far reaching.

There is nothing more important for a person or an organization than full engagement.

Of course, everybody already knows they should be happy at work. But engagement is different from happiness. Being fully engaged means you are motivated to give the extra effort that advances the goals of your employer. Your job might be tough, and it might be stressful, but when you are fully engaged you *want* to do it; you *want* to go the extra mile.

Does this seem unrealistic, or like something you can only find when you have your dream job? If you're a recent graduate, you might be thinking, "Heck, I'd just be grateful for any job right now." If you're a manager, you might think, "Fully engaged? I'd just like my team to show up on time!"

But how often do you actively think about your own career engagement? If you're a manager, how often do you sit down and think about the engagement of your direct reports?

This book will show you that being fully engaged at work has significant implications on all aspects of your life. As an employee of your company, leader of your team, and vital member of your family and circle of friends, you have a *moral obligation* to get to full engagement, and to fully engage those you lead. Unless of course you just don't care about your health, your marriage, or your kids. But we're getting ahead of ourselves. . . .

This book is based on research from Kenexa, a company that conducts employee engagement and opinion surveys for more than 10 million workers in over 150 countries each year. Surprisingly, while the *levels* of engagement vary greatly around the world, we see great commonality among the *drivers* of employee engagement. But this book isn't just based on cold numbers. It is also rooted in our own passion and personal experiences leading teams in the world of work.

Rudy Karsan is the Chairman and CEO of Kenexa, which he cofounded in 1987. Under his leadership, the company has grown from two employees to more than 2,000 with offices in 20 countries. Kenexa solutions help organizations to both hire the best individual for each job and to craft work environments that maximize employee engagement. Kenexa products and services have touched the lives of more than 150 million people.

Kevin Kruse is a former partner at Kenexa and is currently President of Krū Research, with the mission to discover and share the most effective ways to connect with empowered and engaged patients and health consumers. He has built several successful businesses using the strategy of attracting and engaging the very best talent. Both Rudy and Kevin remain lifelong learners of leadership and business as they seek to grow their respective companies and maximize the engagement of their teammates.

The Breakdown

We is split into four parts:

Part One, Career-Life, covers the big picture of how work and jobs have changed over time and how critical they are to overall happiness in life. Specifically, we detail how things like compensation, job choice, and retirement security—all factors in work and life satisfaction—dramatically changed during the Industrial Revolution, but are now shifting back to form a new work-life blend. We also explore the psychological concepts of spillover and crossover to reveal the startling impact job satisfaction has on your life, including your weight and health, the intimacy in your marriage, and even your children's behavior at school.

Part Two, The You in We, is written for the individual and suggests ways that you can actively manage your career, including finding your true purpose, ensuring the right cultural fit with your employer, and managing the growth of your career.

Part Three, How Great Leaders Harmonize Teams, details how employees need to be both *engaged* and *aligned* to reach what we call harmonization. It also explores the impact harmonization has on business performance and financial results.

Part Four, Manager's Toolkit, is a tactical guide written for leaders and managers and is based on an analysis of more than 10 million employee surveys. Here, we reveal the unique drivers that will maximize employee engagement and suggest action steps to improve in these vital areas.

Throughout the book, issues are approached from the *We* perspective, where employer and employees are equal partners in the drive to full engagement. Although many books on leadership and culture put the onus of engagement solely on the employer, and many career-focused books focus solely on the employee, without a comprehensive approach our strategies simply won't work. An employee who does everything right will still be disengaged if he is working for a bad manager. Likewise, the best managers can't engage a person who is working in the wrong job or the wrong industry. *We* must come together, as managers and individuals, to understand the importance of being fully engaged at work and to do what is necessary to foster and maintain that engagement.

You'll also notice that unlike other business books, this one is filled with activities, questions, quizzes, links to online videos, and additional content available online. This is because we love books, but also find them incredibly frustrating. Here's what we mean . . .

We are pathological bibliophiles. We don't just love to read, we actually love books. As a young boy, Kevin's father taught him to treat a book like an egg; a book was not to be dropped or tossed and, of course, never crack the binding! Rudy is an avid reader who is psychologically unable to sell his used books. To make room for new books, he gives away his tomes of knowledge to friends and family, but it would feel sacrilegious to him to ever sell one of his books.

However, despite our personal affection for books, we acknowledge their limitations as a form of communication and persuasion. They just don't stack up well anymore compared to television, the Web, or the newest social media platforms. And even the best books are, by their nature, passive. So what we have created here extends beyond the pages of this book.

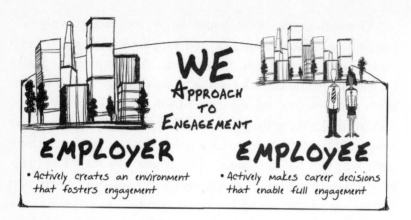

More than a book, *We* is a ticket to an interactive world that includes:

- Online activities that will yield self-discovery and career insights.
- Access to the authors and others in the *We* community via e-mail and social media channels.
- And lastly, a souvenir—a visual reminder—to the idea that the pursuit of full engagement should be top of mind.

Creating a best-selling book is not enough. If we create a best-selling book that rallies a new community of people who are passionate about getting the most out of work, career, and life, then we will have succeeded. To that end, we look forward to connecting with you soon.

We hope to learn from you and your experiences and to continue to share our work in this area. You can connect with us in the following ways:

Web: www.WeTheBook.com

Web: www.KevinKruse.com

Facebook: www.facebook.com\KruseAuthor
Twitter: @Kruse
Twitter: @Kenexa
We hope you enjoy *We* and can't wait to hear from you.

Rudy Karsan and Kevin Kruse
Philadelphia, PA, USA
Summer 2010

Part One

Career-Life

For most of human existence, life may have been hard, but it was simple. We ate what we killed, we reaped what we sowed, and later in history we sold what we made. Life was life. But then a funny thing happened—not coincidentally around the time of the Industrial Revolution. People left their villages and farms and moved to get jobs. And "jobs" became something that we did separate from the rest of our life.

Now, we're shifting back. Societal changes, technology, and our desire to find meaning in what we do is moving us—we should say, returning us—to a Career-Life blend. Although we might wish it weren't so, our jobs and our lives have become deeply intertwined. Your job impacts not just your wealth but also, more importantly, your health, relationships, and overall happiness. To live in harmony you must understand the seismic shifts taking place in the world of work, and how critical your emotions at work are to everything else you do.

1

The Return of the
Work-Life Blend

A successful man continues to look for work even after he has found a job.

—Unknown

Pay to Play in the NBA

You don't have to be a fan of the National Basketball Association (NBA) to appreciate this story about compensation and motivation. . . .

It's a March evening in Dallas, Texas, and the Denver Nuggets have traveled in to play an important basketball game against the Mavericks. The late season NBA game had all the excitement of two big teams fighting for playoff spots, but this game would have special significance for Earl "J.R." Smith, a young Nuggets' player with a knack for landing three-point shots. You see, he knew that on that single night, during that single game, he would earn more money than any other NBA player—a lot more.[1]

It all started when Smith signed a new three-year contract with the Nuggets, which contained a unique clause specifying a performance bonus. If Smith played 2,000 or more minutes in the season, and the Nuggets won 42 or more games, the Nuggets had to pay Smith a very big bonus. At the time of the negotiations, the Nuggets probably thought it was a safe bet. After all, Smith had played less than 1,500 minutes in each of the previous two seasons. But they structured the deal carefully so that he would be both motivated to consistently contribute throughout the year and to value team success as much as his own play time.

Going into this game, Smith had played for a total of 1,991 minutes in the season. Certainly the fans had no idea of the importance of that number and his teammates were probably oblivious to it, too. But there is no doubt that Smith smiled to himself as each minute of the game clock ticked ever closer—1,998 minutes of total game play, 1,999 minutes, 2,000! J.R. Smith, just 23 years old, earned a $600,000 bonus, the highest game-triggered payout ever.

The Return of Variable Pay

Many people hear about professional sports players' multimillion dollar contracts, but few realize that most contracts are built on performance clauses very similar to what the Nuggets owners crafted for J.R. Smith. In baseball, fielders are paid bonuses on the number of *putout assists* and pitchers on the total number of innings pitched. The compensation for an NFL football quarterback is tied to the *quarterback rating*, which is a formula measuring completions, touchdowns, interceptions, and yards gained. In fact, while this "pay for performance" structure may seem odd to today's workers who are used to just being paid for their time, it's actually been the norm in all societies for a long time.

For most of human existence, pay has been tied directly to output. We consumed only what we hunted successfully, later we bartered the crops we harvested and livestock we raised, and still later we would swap the skills we were good at for lodging or meals we needed. Even after the adoption of standardized currencies, we only received it for the goods we made or for specific services (e.g., shoeing a horse). But the industrial revolution and the nature of basic task work inside factories quickly broadened the practice of paying for time rather than performance. Unskilled factory workers were paid wages by the week or by the day, with many people working as many as 16 hours in a 24-hour period. Factory managers were paid by the week. In the 1800s, the English labor movement rallied around a pay-for-time slogan: "A Fair Day's Wages for a Fair Day's Work." In the 1900s, a new army of white-collar office workers began receiving salaries based on annual estimates of time worked.

This two-century long experiment in fixed-payment-for-fixed-time peaked in the 1930s.[2] Then slowly but surely, more and more corporations began to introduce *variable pay* programs for at least part of their workforce. Variable pay refers to compensation systems where a large part of total compensation is performance based, and must be re-earned each year. It is typically tied to the performance of the individual, that person's team, the employer, or some combination of the three. Payment can be made in cash or sometimes in stock options or stock grants in the company.

Funding for variable pay programs is now dramatically rising. Figure 1.1 shows how the portion of compensation tied to variable pay has tripled in the last 20 years, increasing from 4.2 percent in 1990 to 12 percent in 2009.[3]

By the year 2030, we project that fully one-quarter of white-collar pay will be tied to performance and output. This data reflects nonsales compensation; if you were to include sales

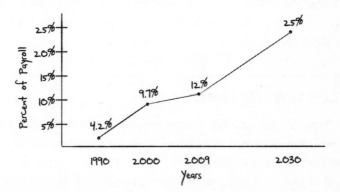

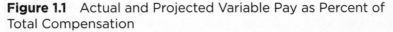

Figure 1.1   Actual and Projected Variable Pay as Percent of Total Compensation

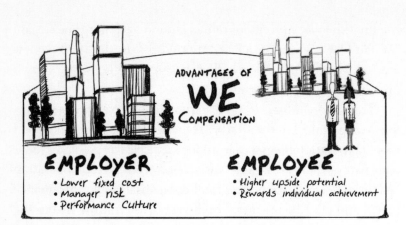

Figure 1.2 Advantages of "We Compensation"

commissions, these numbers would be in the 35 percent of total pay range.

This dramatic shift to variable pay is an example of We principles at work (see Figure 1.2). Employers benefit from variable pay as it better enables them to manage base costs, reduce risks from unforeseen events, and reward employees whose efforts directly drive business outcomes. Workers benefit from variable pay programs because it can increase their compensation each year far beyond cost-of-living increases and better reward their individual efforts.

Case Study: The Kenexa Z-Index

So how do you actually implement an effective variable pay plan? How do you balance the organization's goals with the performance of the individual?

At Kenexa, more than 2,000 employees track something called the "Z-Index." It's a single number that boils down the organization's top goals into a single score.

Z-Index = (Sales Backlog + Priority Partner Program Revenue + Enterprise Sales) × Income Percentage × Renewal Rate

This internally is simplified as:

$$Z = (B + P^3 + E) \times I \times R$$

The factors that comprise the Z-Index reflect the strategic priorities of the company. Sales backlog represents what's been sold and committed to, but not yet delivered or earned. Enterprise Sales is a measure of total revenue, P^3 is the revenue from the Priority Partner Program, which represents top clients, the contract renewal rate reflects client satisfaction, and income percentage reflects the value of profit. From Rudy in his office near Philadelphia, PA, to the office workers in Vizag, India, and everybody in between, the Z-Index makes crystal clear that Kenexa values profitable growth and client service.

The Z-Index offers a precise answer to the question, "How are we doing as a company?" The Z-Index formula is taught to all new hires, and is reinforced with prominent placement in internal newsletters, posters, and the company's Intranet, and leaders frequently speak to the score in their team meetings.

Targets are set at the beginning of the year with the Gold Z-Score representing the most ambitious goal, a Silver Z-Score is equal to 90 percent of the gold level, and a Bronze Z-Score reflects 80 percent of the gold level goal (i.e., the bronze goal is 20 percent less than the highest gold-level target). Kenexa senior leadership receives a base pay compensation that is only a fraction of their potential total. The majority of their compensation is variable pay that is tied to both company performance against the Z-Index, and their individual performance against their quarterly and annual objectives. Based on the success of this variable pay plan, compensation plans tied to the Z-Index are being rolled out through the rest of Kenexa.

Managers can use variable pay plans as a powerful tool to attract and retain top talent. For individuals, it offers a higher income potential based on one's unique talents. Variable pay plans must be designed to balance synergistic interests, just as the contracts of professional athletes reward for both team and individual performance. If a basketball player was only rewarded for three-point shots, he may choose to shoot when he should really pass. If a quarterback was rewarded only for the number of games played, he might choose to avoid hard tackles with a slide instead of diving for the first down. J.R. Smith earned his bonus only if he played a certain number of minutes (the individual goal) *and* the Denver Nuggets won at least 42 games (the team goal). We-compensation balances the goals of the organization with the goals of the individual.

So Many Jobs

What is most striking about this simple word is that despite 100,000 years of human social evolution, the word *job* has only been around for the last 400 years. For most of human history, people had one job; they were hunter-gatherers. They moved about from place to place to forage edible plants and hunt game. Eventually, about 12,000 years ago, they learned to domesticate edible plants and animals, thus enabling simple settlements and eventually, they became farmers. Even as settlements flourished and grew in population, most people either tended their crops or were considered herdsmen, moving their cows and sheep across different fields to graze.[4]

With the Bronze and Iron Ages (approximately 3000 to 500 B.C.) came only a few more job types. Most people were still farmers, but smiths and smelters spent their time turning copper into bronze, traders traveled great distances to barter metals and gemstones, craftsmen built chariots and boats, and professional

> ## Definition of Job
>
> Job
> Function: Noun
> Data: circa 1627
> Definition: a small, miscellaneous piece of work undertaken on order at a stated rate
> Or, a specific duty, role, or function
>
> —*Merriam-Webster Online Dictionary*[5]

warriors protected the traders. By the time of Ancient Rome job choice expanded slightly and included priests, scribes, and with an intentional misuse of the word *job*, you also had slaves. About 1,000 years ago, in the Middle Ages, you could find more service jobs like doctor, bookkeeper, butler, maid, cook, groundskeeper, page, and even minstrel entertainers.

But a historic shift in what we did to make a living occurred when the first steam engine was unveiled in 1769 and the Industrial Revolution ushered in the word *job* as we know it today. Power generation increasingly came from coal engines rather than animals and rapid wealth generation came from owning factories, not land. People living in the country flocked to cities as factory owners hired unskilled commoditized workers to run the machines. A salary report from an 1860 silk mill in England shows just a sample of the brand new industrial job types including loom cleaners, winders, twisters, weavers, and gauze examiners. The explosion in jobs and new job types was unprecedented, and the burst in factory workers, of course, ushered in a new class of managers as well.[6]

There was another shift in the 1930s, which was reflected by the American writer Upton Sinclair when he coined the term *white-collar worker* to describe the proliferation of a new

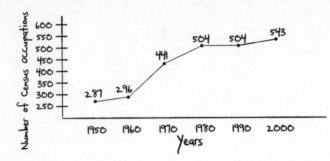

Figure 1.3   Number of Job Categories in the U.S. Census

class of office workers. These service jobs included sales, marketing, finance, customer service, civil service, teaching, and other nonmanual labor positions. The number of white-collar workers outstripped blue-collar workers and farmers by the mid-1950s, and in turn, has been supplanted by *knowledge workers* in the new information age.

This short traipse through occupational history shows how for thousands of years we've only had a handful of job possibilities but in very recent times, we've seen an explosion in job types. In fact, the 1950 U.S. Census listed 287 job categories and a mere 50 years later, it lists 543 job types—a net increase of 83 percent[7] (see Figure 1.3).

Disappearing Jobs

In the 1967 film *The Graduate*, Benjamin Braddock (played by a young Dustin Hoffman) is anxious and confused about his future. In a classic film scene, an older family friend named Mr. McGuire offers some unsolicited career advice.

Mr. McGuire:	I just want to say one word to you—just one word.
Ben:	Yes sir.

Mr. McGuire:	Are you listening?
Ben:	Yes I am.
Mr. McGuire:	Plastics.
Ben:	Exactly how do you mean?
Mr. McGuire:	There's a great future in plastics. Think about it. Will you think about it?

The single word *plastics* is viewed by many as the most famous line ever delivered in an American movie.

Previous generations marched with confidence into their careers. Often people chose to pursue the same careers their parents pursued. They assumed that a good job in a good company would guarantee their future. One worried about climbing the ladder, not whether the ladder would tip over. We have long since left the days when career advice could be summed up in a single word (e.g., plastics), no matter how bright the prospects for a specific industry may seem. No longer can we assume that we will have to learn just one trade, or choose just one employer, or even just one industry. A job for life is the very rare exception, not the rule.

Case Study: Typesetting Industry

Before the mid-1980s, everything from business cards to display ads were designed by special typesetting companies with employees whose skills ranged from typography to photography and film, as well as working the press itself. With the advent of affordable personal computers and desktop publishing software, in less than a decade the typesetting industry almost disappeared. Professional printers who thought they

(continued)

(continued)

had skills that would employ them for life found themselves in early retirement, getting little from their bankrupt unions.

During this time of rapid change, who do you think fared better—those who mastered the typesetting machines, or those who mastered visual design? Those who worked the press, or those who sold the printing? Or, to put in other terms, those who assumed nothing would ever change, or those who were naturally curious and had a love for learning (maybe even learning about this new thing called the Macintosh)?

The visual artist Raymon Elozua created a powerful chronicle of jobs that no longer exist in his self-published book, *Lost Labor*. You can view over 100 photographs of jobs that no longer exist on his Web site, www.lostlabor.com, including rubber reclaimers, hat makers, poultry pluckers, ice haulers, and many more.

Being engaged at work doesn't mean being blissfully ignorant of today's business realities. Rapid change means true security comes from actively managing your career, not assuming you made the one right job choice. It is not the employer's role alone to ease your anxieties; it is dangerous to ever cede control over your future to someone else. If industries change, you must change with them. Some skills are more transferable than others. We explore later in the book the importance of being a continual learner. But paramount to being a continual learner is to constantly look at your career path, your industry, and the possible options in the future.

If you are a manager, it should be part of your job to assist your team members in their career path planning as well. You of course are already grooming your own replacement and have a succession plan in place (right?). But all your team members will benefit

Figure 1.4 "We" Approach to Career Pathing

in their current job if they see a future in the company through job promotions and variety (see Figure 1.4).

From Job, to Jobs

Michael, age 55, packs up his laptop, grabs his car keys, and nods to his boss as he leaves the office just after five. With an advanced degree in biostatistics, Michael earns a handsome six-figure salary writing clinical trial reports for his employer, a leading biotech company in California. But Michael doesn't drive straight home. He stops at 16-year-old Jenna's house. You see, Jenna is struggling with advanced algebra and the big SAT exam is coming up. Michael greets Jenna's parents before pulling out his calculator, asking Jenna to do the same, and sitting down for his "second shift."

Tutoring could never replace his day job of course, but Michael found that the science-oriented parents in the valley paid well for an hour of his time. And while he wouldn't do it for free, it feels good helping kids get better at math and several of their parents have become new

*friends. You'd think Michael would be too burned out from his day job
to want to spend an hour teaching math—but to his own surprise, it
actually invigorates him. He feels refreshed by the time he gets home.*

Another strong workforce trend is the shift to holding more
than just one job. The predictions made by many a decade ago
are becoming reality. Irish business guru Charles Handy, in his
2001 book *The Elephant and the Flea*, coined the term *the portfolio
life* to describe those who juggle multiple roles and occupations.
Similar to how one builds an investment portfolio, Handy pre-
dicted that more people would assemble multiple jobs to reduce
risk, maximize interest, and allow for more flexible schedules and
work-life balance. The very same year, Daniel Pink suggested we
would become a "Free Agent Nation" in the book of the same
name, in order to become more fulfilled with our work, and to
take back more of our time.

And it's not just people in lower income brackets who are jug-
gling multiple jobs. CEOs and senior executives of large companies
frequently also hold paid director positions with other companies,
not to mention unpaid roles with nonprofit organizations. For
example, in 2009 IBM CEO Samuel Palmisano earned $1.8 million
in salary from IBM, but also earned about $100,000 as a director for
ExxonMobil.[8] Zachary Carter is a partner at the law firm Dorsey &
Whitney, but also earns $425,000 as a director for Cablevision and
another $90,000 as a director for March & McLennan.[9]

Today's professional athletes don't just get paid to play the
game; the most successful ones sign endorsement deals, some give
speeches, and others sell autographs. In fact, the world's highest
paid athletes earned much more from "moonlighting" than from
their day jobs. In 2009, golfer Tiger Woods made $7.7 million
in salary and winnings, but made $92 million in endorsements.
LeBron James made $14 million for playing basketball, but another
$28 million in endorsements. Dale Earnhardt Jr. was paid $4.6
million for racing, and another $22 million in endorsements.[10]

The U.S. Bureau of Labor Statistics actually measures the number of multiple jobholders in its monthly census, which stood at 5.2 percent of all workers in 2009.[11] But we think this number is vastly underreported. Their measurement is based on this question: "*Last week*, did you have more than one job (or business), including part-time, evening, or weekend work?"[12] Many multiple jobholders might not think to answer yes to this category, if their second job is not one considered to be conventional. They include the executives who work on corporate boards perhaps only one day a month and get paid on a quarterly basis; moonlighting-entrepreneurs who will take their income in the form of profits at the end of the year; members of multilevel marketing companies who are paid only when they hold parties or reach certain milestones; consultants who typically work for several different employers on multiple projects, but may consider being a consultant "one job." And of course, there are many, many others who work on a cash basis, and would never dream of telling the government that indeed, they held more than one job in the prior week.

We actually wonder who doesn't hold more than one job these days. Just considering our own positions, Rudy's multiple jobs include duties as the CEO of Kenexa along with being a director at other companies, while Kevin is President of Krū Research, is on the board of a bank, and is a professional speaker. Among our friends and family alone we know:

- A pharmaceutical purchasing director who also owns and oversees 20 rental properties.
- A real estate broker who owns a restaurant.
- A sheriff's officer who also works as a personal trainer.
- A lawyer who is a partner in a medical device startup.
- A teacher who runs a summer tutoring camp.
- A commercial property manager who also runs a cleaning service.

- Several primary care doctors who also deliver paid lectures and serve as paid expert witnesses in malpractice cases.
- A high-end private security guard who is occasionally called again for duty as a U.S. Navy SEAL.
- An accountant who runs an ice cream store.
- An office manager who does accounting for a print shop.
- A sales manager who is also a successful day trader.

Why are so many people holding more than one job?

- Income—Perhaps the biggest benefit, of course, is that it can increase your income.
- Variety—Second jobs often don't pay much, but they enable the worker to learn new skills, meet new people, and do interesting work.
- Diversification—Having more than one employer or source of income can reduce the financial and emotional impact of losing your primary job, and may enable you to more quickly recover by growing the secondary job.
- Flexibility—For some, having two part-time jobs offers the same income as one full-time job, but enables them to fulfill other role duties like picking up their kids from the bus stop or caring for an elderly parent.
- Risk Elimination—Many entrepreneurs began building their business while they still maintained their day job. Knowing that the first couple years of a startup can be very lean, maintaining the primary job until things are more stable reduces the risk of entrepreneurship.

Of course, along with these many benefits comes an increase in work-related time commitments and great responsibility, too.

Having more than one job is neither better nor worse—but it is a rapidly growing trend. As an individual, you should consider whether or not becoming a multiple jobholder would enable you to develop new skills, supplement income, or reduce career risk. As a manager or employer, you need to acknowledge that you can win the fight for the best talent by focusing on their productivity and less on being their only source of income.

How to Negotiate a Multi-Job Career

You might be thinking, "I'd love to have multiple jobs but my employer would never let me do it."

Indeed, the most important thing is to be completely transparent and open about your situation. You'd never want to be in the situation where you bump into your boss when you're working your second job. If you're employed full-time, what your boss should care most about is that your primary attention is with your primary job and that your other activities won't interfere in any way.

Go to www.WeTheBook.com to watch "Negotiate a Multi-Job Career: An Interview with Rudy Karsan" to see how to address the multiple job issue during a job interview, or with your existing employer.

From 9-to-5 to Get-It-Done

As we've shifted to a knowledge-based economy, with business being conducted around the world, the notion of a 9 AM to 5 PM standard workday has become antiquated. Perhaps a better description is *short lived*. After all, historically people just worked whatever hours it took to get the job done. Hunt and gather when your family or tribe needed food. Get up early to milk the cows and do the heavy work before the hot afternoon sun rose. Shoe the horse when the traveler stops by and pays you to.

Many are surprised to learn that the standard 40-hour work-week only came into existence in the United States recently, in 1938, with the passage of the Fair Labor Standards Act. Although many had fought for a shorter, defined workweek throughout the 1800s, it was actually the Great Depression that enabled passage of the act; with fewer hours per worker, companies would be forced to keep more workers employed. Today, according to one recent survey, 63 percent of Americans are working more than 40 hours per week and 40 percent are working more than 50 hours per week.[13]

More relevant, it's not the total number of hours worked (there has always been the notion of overtime) but it's the set time and location of work that is noticeably disappearing. Work is increasingly bleeding into and blending into the rest of our lives. With e-mail, laptops, and smart phones, we are increasingly blending work activities with leisure activities. Who hasn't checked in with the office while standing at their child's bus stop? Who hasn't sent an e-mail or two out while standing on the sidelines of their kids' sports practice or game? Left a little early to take their spouse to the theater and made up the time Sunday night when the kids went to bed?

This return to a work-life blend is a natural result of dual-income families benefiting from more flexible work hours, and from companies that benefit from higher service levels and the ability to conduct business across multiple time zones. It has also been enabled by advances in communication technology; smart phones let us text, talk, e-mail, and run applications from anywhere while broadband connections and Wi-Fi keep us connected to work from our home offices.

There's even a management movement known as Results Only Work Environment (ROWE), which emerged from Best Buy's experiment in extreme work flexibility. The idea is that employees can work when they want and where they want, as long as the work gets done. What Best Buy, and others who are emulating them, have found, is that productivity goes up and turnover goes down.

Retirement (In)Security

On January 31, 1940, Ida Mae Fuller became an unlikely character for American history books. "Aunt Ida," as her friends called her, was born on a Vermont farm in 1874. She never married, and worked for many years as a schoolteacher and later as a legal secretary. She retired in 1939 and while running errands in the town of Rutland, Vermont, decided to stop by one of the government offices. As she tells it, "It wasn't that I expected anything, mind you, but I knew I'd been paying for something called Social Security and I wanted to ask the people in Rutland about it."

Three months after putting in her request, Ida Fuller would become the first person to receive a Social Security check, number 00-000-001. It was in the amount of $22.54. Although she only ever paid in $24.75 into the Social Security system, she would go on to live until the age of 100 and collect $22,888.92 in retirement payments.[14]

Throughout history, humans have always faced difficult times related to illness, disability, and the inability to work in old age. In the earliest times, we depended on our families for economic security. We cared for our elderly parents just as they cared for us when we were children. Farms were passed down among the generations; whoever owned land would never go hungry. As farms gave way to villages in the Middle Ages, craftsmen banded together to form guilds and guild members collectively replaced the security that was previously provided by family and assets.

About 400 years ago, for the first time in the Western world, people began to turn over these kinds of responsibilities to the state. The "Poor Laws" were passed in England, which instituted new taxes to fund welfare for the poor and English settlers brought their notions of state-guaranteed welfare with them to America. But through the 1800s, relief was made as unpleasant as possible in order to discourage dependency. Those who received welfare from the state lost their personal property, lost the right to vote, and in some cases were marked with a "P" on their clothing so all could see that they received welfare for the poor.

But the 1930s brought the Great Depression with huge corporate losses, the collapse of the stock market, and massive unemployment. The impact on the elderly was especially harsh. These extreme circumstances led to widespread pleas for government help, and President Roosevelt called for the formation of the program of Social Security. The original program was quite basic: only people who paid into the system received benefits, the retirement age was 65, and the payouts were modest.[15]

When Should *You* Receive Social Security?

In 1935, a 20-year-old worker could expect to live to age 67. This means he could expect that Social Security would provide modest support for the last two years of his life. If we applied the original standards to our life expectancy today, we wouldn't be eligible for Social Security until age 75.[16]

Over time, the Social Security program has grown considerably:

- Benefits were granted to the spouse and children of deceased workers
- The value of benefits doubled in the 1950s as Congress made inflation-related adjustments

- Disability benefits were added in the 1950s
- Early retirement features enabled workers to retire at 62

Today, one in seven Americans receives Social Security benefits and by 2037, the money will run out—one century after it was started.[17] It's impossible to predict exactly what changes will be made to save the program, but it is likely that the retirement age will be extended, we will have to pay higher taxes into the system, and benefits will only be paid to those who pass some form of means testing (i.e., those who have accumulated a certain level of assets will not be able to draw back Social Security).

In addition to government-run retirement security, a parallel phenomenon occurred with the rapid growth of employer-sponsored pensions. Private pension plans were very rare until after World War II. But then they grew quickly to the point where by 1999, fully 44 percent of all workers in the United States were part of employer pension plans.[18] These were predominantly *defined benefit* plans, whereby the employer alone pays into the system and guarantees retirement payments to the worker for life. The problem with these plans, of course, is that while the payout is a promised and fixed amount, the contribution the company puts into the program and what happens to their investment over time is variable.

Indeed many companies made promises they couldn't keep, and many companies and their pension programs have gone bust. In 1964, carmaker Studebaker closed down after 60 years in business, and 4,500 workers lost 85 percent of their promised pension. In response to the Studebaker crisis and others like it, the U.S. Congress passed the Employee Retirement Income Security Act (ERISA) of 1974 and established the Pension Benefit Guarantee Corporation (PBGC) to regulate and insure pension plans. But the looming pension crisis—with unfunded benefits in the trillions of dollars—is far bigger than the PBGC can handle. Experts talk not *if* the PBGC will need a government bailout but *when* it will need a bailout.

When it comes to retirement security, in as little as 100 years, we've shifted responsibility from ourselves and our families to governments and employers. This turned out to be risky as neither companies nor governments can fund the promises that have now been made. For many, sadly, there will be no pension at all and for others, they'll receive a fraction of what was to be expected.

Defined benefit plans—plans supported by and controlled by employers—are risky, underfunded, and are now seen by most as an ill-conceived experiment. The *We* approach to retirement security is one in which there is shared responsibility and control (see Figure 1.5). These defined contribution plans, most commonly in the form of 401(k) plans, shift the model whereby employees must pay in a percentage of their pay, employers match the contribution, and government gives up potential tax revenues

Figure 1.5 "We" Retirement Plans

on the investment income. Additionally, 401(k)s empower the participant to take the plan with them when they leave the company—no longer do you need to work for 10, 20, or 30 years for your pension to kick in. While critics of defined contribution plans often say that this shifts too much risk to the employee, we would suggest that trusting that your employer is going to fully fund your plan and still be around to pay it out is the riskiest option of all. Just ask the workers at Studebaker.

From Work-Life Balance to the Work-Life Blend

As our history has shown, we've existed for more than 100,000 years living a certain way. We knew everybody in our community, job choices were limited, we perfected our chosen craft throughout our lives, we consumed what we produced, our home and workplace were often one and the same, and when we got too old to work we would be supported by family or charity.

Then, very recently, the steam engine was invented and things dramatically changed. We left our families and moved to work in big factories in bigger cities where we became anonymous. We began to sell our time instead of our output. We expected a job for life and let our retirement become somebody else's responsibility. We separated work from life. The thrill of the hunt was replaced with the malaise of entitlement. However, we painfully discovered in the last 50 years that both our job and our retirement are always at risk, and we are foolish to cede responsibility for them to anybody but ourselves.

The Industrial Revolution brought us great societal wealth, but it may have come at the price of individual happiness. The Surgeon General estimates that 16 percent of the U.S. adult population suffers from some form of anxiety,[19] and one in 10 American adults is now taking antidepressant drugs.[20]

If you take just one message away from this book, make it this: the idea that work and life are separate entities is an illusion. Everything is your life. And you spend far too much time "at work" for it not to be an enjoyable, fulfilling, and yes, an engaging experience. But the *We* approach is one that says stop striving for a work-life *balance*, and begin to craft a work-life *blend*.

The *We* mind-set is about recognizing and accepting the world as it really is, and assuming shared responsibility for your career and financial success. We are living longer than ever before, with more job churn and job choices, and much less financial security. It is just as foolish to believe happiness comes from the dichotomy of the work-life balance as it is to think we can all return to a hunter-gatherer existence. The answer is to do away with the false duality of work and life, and to embrace a work-life *blend*. This requires us to reject the false choice between work and life, career and family, and fun and money.

We began this chapter highlighting the performance pay of a professional basketball player, and from pro athletes we can see clues as to how to succeed in this new world of the work-life blend. They receive variable pay based on both individual and team performance. They hold multiple jobs, playing for teams but also working endorsement deals. They know they will retire in their mid-30s or early 40s, depending on the sport, so they plan for multiple careers—planning ahead for a time when they may go into announcing, or opening a restaurant, or real estate development. While our day job may not involve hitting a sinking fastball, we can certainly learn from the career paths and career mind-sets of these athletes. And we must remember to be passionate whatever the game is that we are playing.

Chapter Summary

The Return of the Work-Life Blend

(You can download this summary as a one-page PDF at www .WeTheBook.com.)

The path to career success and full engagement is made easier once you understand the forces in the world of work, and that it's now a *new* world of work. As a species, for 100,000 years we made no distinction between our life and our work, and the word *job* didn't even exist. The Industrial Revolution brought great societal wealth but introduced the idea that work and life were separate from one another, and our pay was tied to time rather than our production. But the pendulum is now swinging back in the other direction, and we can see a shift:

- From pay-for-time to pay-for-performance
- From limited job choices to complex and numerous job choices
- From holding one job to being a multiple jobholder
- From false guarantees to shared responsibility for economic security

Key Takeaways for Individuals

- You will be working longer, and in more jobs, than ever before.
- Therefore, it's critical that you find a career and job that fully engages you.
- You must cast off any entitlement thinking you may have and become mindful of your career and long-term success.

(*continued*)

(*continued*)

Key Takeaways for Managers

- Developing your skills as a manager is a way to reduce career risk, as leadership skills are in demand across all industries.
- Selling the flexibility that comes with a work-life blend model will enable you to recruit and retain top talent.
- Offering a variable-pay structure can both reduce your budget risk while motivating your top performers.

Chapter Bonus Material

Video Interview with Rudy Karsan

You have special access to material only available to readers of this book. Watch this exclusive and provocative interview with Rudy Karsan as he goes into more detail about the dangers of entitlement thinking.

1. Go to www.WeTheBook.com.
2. Click the "Bonus Material" button/link.
3. Click the link that says "Entitlement Thinking."
4. Enter the password "security" (without the quotation marks).

Enjoy your bonus material!

2

Profits Drop When Your Spouse Kicks the Dog

Do something you love and you will never work a day in your life.

—Confucius

Activity: Your Thoughts on Work

So what do you think about work? Go ahead, be honest. Tell us what you think by completing Activity 2.1. We won't tell anyone your answers.

Activity 2.1 View of Work

INSTRUCTIONS: Consider each of these five commonplace statements about work. Reflect on how much you agree with the sentiment of the statement and circle the number that most closely matches your level of agreement or disagreement.

	Strongly Disagree		Neutral		Strongly Agree
"I'm working for the weekend."	1	2	3	4	5
"I work to live, not live to work."	1	2	3	4	5
"Nobody ever lies on their deathbed wishing they had spent more time at work."	1	2	3	4	5
"Thank God it's Friday!"	1	2	3	4	5

(*continued*)

31

Activity 2.1 (continued)

	Strongly Disagree		Neutral		Strongly Agree
"I'll do this job for five or ten years, save my money, then quit and do what I really want to do."	1	2	3	4	5

Calculate Your Total Score

Instructions: Simply add up all the numbers you circled

= _____

SCORE: If your score is 20 points or higher, boy are we glad you're reading this book! It means you don't yet realize just how critical your job is in other areas of your life, and you're probably not very excited about the job you have now. If your score is between 11 and 19 you are probably like most people; you know you spend a lot of time at work, and you want to like your job, but you still may not realize just how vital work is to your overall life experience. If your total score is less than 10, that's great. It means you already know that work is an important part of life, and you want to be engaged. It is our hope that the pages to follow will reinforce this view and motivate you to pursue maximum engagement.

All of the statements above reflect a belief that work is separate from the rest of our lives. That we can somehow lock it up or get rid of it on the weekend, or that we can take it off like a pair of muddy shoes before we walk into our homes. But the reality is that even if we are on the job from 9 to 5—or probably far longer—work doesn't leave us when we leave the office.

Step Right Up!

"Step right up and gather round," the nineteenth-century traveling medicine man shouted. "Have I got an ointment just for you! And for you and you! The contents of this bottle were made with the venom from 50 rattlesnakes. Sir, rub three drops on your elbows and knees and your joint pain will disappear. Sir, I say Sir! Are you hard of hearing? One drop in each ear will fix you right up. And Madame, for your unique feminine ailments . . ."

Today's snake oil salesmen have moved the pitch from the back of a wagon to Web sites and infomercials. Many people now pay for books, audio programs, or DVDs to learn some secret that they believe will bring them health, wealth, and love. We all seem to want to lose weight, find a mate, make money, and of course, live happily ever after. And in this chapter, we give you powerful information that can actually help you achieve all this and more. Like the snake oil salesmen, our claims are bold; they will change your life. But what we are offering isn't snake oil and it doesn't come in a bottle. It's not a secret either; it's been proven in hundreds of rigorous studies. Quite simply, we are selling the idea that *your job matters*. More specifically, how engaged you are at work counts more than you may realize.

But before we prove how essential engagement at work is to you, we use our best carnival barker voice to summon you to step right up and see what's possible:

- Want to lose weight? Be fully engaged at work.
- Want to live longer? Be fully engaged at work.
- Want a better marriage? Be fully engaged at work.
- Want to be a better parent? Be fully engaged at work.
- Want to achieve inner happiness? Be fully engaged at work.

Hard to believe? Read on.

Roles, Identities, and Work

We don't often pause and ask ourselves, "Who am I?" And if you uttered that question out loud a few times you'd probably be rushed to the nearest hospital. But it's an important question. Your identity, or perceived role in life, is what gives you daily purpose and guides your behaviors. If you view yourself as a loyal friend, you might be more likely to return a friend's call quickly or perhaps help them move their couch upstairs. If you view yourself as a civic-minded activist, you might be more likely to engage in a protest or donate to a politician's re-election campaign.

And, of course, we have more than one identity, more than one role. You might think of yourself as a parent and a spouse, a war veteran and an artist. In fact, before we go any further, consider some of the identities listed in Activity 2.2. This activity will help you gain some insights into your own identity.

Activity 2.2 Importance of Various Role-Identities

(You can also complete this activity online at www.WeTheBook.com)

> INSTRUCTIONS:
>
> STEP 1: Put a check mark in column A, next to each role that you identify with.
>
> STEP 2: In column B, rank how important each role that you checked is in your life. For example, if you are a parent and that's most important to you, put the number "1" in column B adjacent to parent, then put "2" in the role that is second in importance, and so on.
>
> STEP 3: Now think about how much time you spend each week in any given role, and write the time estimate in column C. For example, for the worker/employee role just add up how

Activity 2.2 (continued)

much time on average you spend working and on work-related activities. For parent or spouse, put the actual time you spend with your kids or your partner.C. For example, for the worker/employee role just add up how much time on average you spend working and on work-related activities. For parent or spouse, put the actual time you spend with your kids or your partner.

	A Identify	B Importance	C Time per Week
Parent			
Spouse/Mate			
Friend			
Religious Observer			
Worker/Employee			
Son/Daughter			
Relative			
Neighbor			
Student			
In-law			
Group Member			
Athlete			
Hobbyist			
Volunteer			
Caregiver			

Spoiler alert! Make sure to do the above exercise, because we're about to reveal the results of a real-world experiment based on a similar exercise.

This role and ranking exercise is similar to one used in a study by Peggy Thoits, a sociologist at Indiana University.

You might have noticed that the roles listed in Activity 2.2 aren't listed in alphabetical order. They are listed in the order of importance according to Thoits' interviews with 700 working adults. In this study, most of the participants indicated that being a parent was the most important role they held in their lives, spouse was ranked as the second most important role, friend third, and so on. What's most interesting is that people listed "worker" in the fifth position, right below being a religious observer.[1]

Think carefully about these questions:

- Did you rank the importance of your roles in a similar manner to others?
- How important is the worker/employee identity to you?
- Did you also rank "worker/employee" in the fifth position, or maybe even lower?

Look at column C where you indicated how much time you spend in each role. Notice a bit of a mismatch between the time spent in each role and its order of importance? We aren't suggesting that they should completely match; being a parent might be the most important role, but your teenage kids certainly don't want you spending 60 hours a week with them. But if you are spending so much more time as a worker than in the other roles, it should be easy to see how one's employment plays a critical part in who you are and how you experience life.

What's in a Name?

Read each statement in Activity 2.3 and indicate whether you agree with it or not.

Activity 2.3 Influences on Identity

INSTRUCTIONS: Read each statement below and indicate whether you agree or disagree.

Who I am today has been shaped by my parents.	Disagree	Agree
Who I am today has been shaped by the places where I have lived.	Disagree	Agree
Who I am today has been shaped by my physical appearance.	Disagree	Agree
Who I am today has been shaped by my job.	Disagree	Agree

INTERPRETATION: Most people who answer these statements agree with the first three. Many don't realize the strong link between our personal identity and the work we do.

We know that our parents have a lot to do with who we are. After all, they're typically the ones to teach us how to walk, how to talk, and directly or indirectly, how to feel about different things and how to react. There is a reason why the stereotypical psychologist always says, "So tell me about your mother."

Most people also readily see how where they were born and raised—or where they've spent the majority of their time—has a large impact on who they are today. Somebody born and raised in Nairobi, Kenya, will have a different outlook on life and make different choices than someone born and raised in London, England. Someone who spent a lifetime in San Francisco is likely to have a worldview different from a person who has lived his or her entire life in Birmingham, Alabama.

Although less obvious, our physical traits may impact our personality and choices. If we think we are unattractive, we may be socially awkward or less confident, and indeed there could be workplace biases against us. If we are bigger than average or athletically gifted, we may become more sports oriented and competitive during our teen years. There are in fact some jobs that require a certain height, fitness score, or physical capability (e.g., pilot, fire fighter, package delivery).

I sometimes think I was born to live up to my name. How could I be anything else but what I am, having been named Madonna? I would either have ended up a nun or this.
—Madonna (born Madonna Louise Ciccone),
quoted in *Elle*, 2001

The fourth statement is one where there is less agreement. My identity is shaped by my job? Yes. In fact, over the last century and increasingly over the last 500 years, one's occupation has often been the primary way a person is identified by others.

Your full name reflects your family and cultural heritage. It makes up a part of our identity and is often the source of personal and family pride. Family names, or surnames, only came into use about 700 to 1,000 years ago. Before that they just weren't necessary. One of the most unique parts of one's identity, his or her name, has a variety of origins, including occupation-based roots. With fewer people, and less travel, you pretty much knew everyone in your village or tribe by using just one name. But eventually, the nobility or rulers in the country started adding surnames, followed by the merchants, and eventually even commoners and farmers took surnames, too. With few exceptions, surnames have four origins:

1. Patronymic names—These are names indicating who your father was. The name John Davidson was at one time "John the son of David." The Irish used Mac for this purpose—Ian

MacCarthy was "Ian the son of Carthy." The suffix *-iak* in Polish means son of (e.g., Wozniak). In Spanish, *-ez* indicates son of (e.g., Hernandez). Arabic names don't follow the given name, middle name, family name format and instead are comprised of a whole chain of names showing lineage on the father's side of the family. The name "Muhammad *bin Nidh'aal bin* Akins" means "Muhammad, son-of-Nidhaal, son-of-Akins."

2. Location names—Another common practice was to take a name that described where you were from. This could be really local, indicating that you lived on a hill or in a glen, or quite broad, denoting what state or region you are from. Andrew who lives in York became Andrew York. The Chinese surname Chiang refers to a feudal territory and the name Hong is a political district. Naming practices in India vary widely but in Southern India, the name of the village has commonly formed the surname.

3. Trait names—Though not always flattering, many surnames originated from one's most notable physical trait. If you stood out with red hair you'd likely have been given the name Reid in England, Rousseau in France, or Roth in Germany. Or maybe your stature earned you "Longfellow" or "Petit." Trait names can also come from personality traits. Part of your Arabic name might be *al-Salam*, which means "the peacemaker" or *al-Hakim*, "the wise."

4. Occupation names—Historians suggest that occupation-derived surnames came later. Although occupation-based names are still rare in many Eastern cultures, you can find examples of them in China and India, and even Arabic names sometimes have a *nisba* (i.e., a name's suffix) that refers to an occupation. Of course, occupation-based last names can be seen most frequently in the Western world. This took root

with English names in the Middle Ages. To differentiate among the different Johns in the village, you would refer to one as "John the Baker" and another as "John the Mason." Table 2.1 shows many common English occupation names.

In a much earlier age of apprenticeships, it would not be uncommon for a blacksmith's son to become a Smith, or for a banker's son to become a Banker.

But of course, we've long since broken this limited loop where the job indicates the name, and your name (and father) encourages your career choice. Mick Jagger isn't exactly known for selling fish. But we are about to see that this link between job and identity isn't completely broken. You, your life, and your job continue to be tightly intertwined.

Just as work intertwines with identity, emotions at work entangle with other areas of your life.

Table 2.1   Common English Occupation Names

Brewster (brewer)
Carter (transported goods)
Chapman (shopkeeper)
Chandler (candlemaker)
Clark (clerk)
Cooper (barrel maker)
Crocker (potter)
Fletchers (maker of bows and arrows)
Jagger (fish peddler)
Mason (bricklayer)
Porter (doorkeeper)
Smith (blacksmith)
Tanner (turns hides into leather)

Spillover and Crossover

Kevin once received what he considers to be the ultimate work compliment. It didn't actually come from a colleague—it came from the wife of one of his team members. She said, "I really want to thank you. You made my marriage better." Now, at the time Kevin didn't know much about the notion of spillover so he was a bit confused and speechless. "Paul used to be such a grump," she continued. "Since going to work for you he's like a new man. I actually like having him around the house now."

You have a bad day at work and come home and kick the dog. That's the classic example of what psychologists call the *spillover effect*. This implies that your work-related emotions spill over into other areas of your life. It's easy to understand and even if you don't have a dog, it's probably an experience with which you're familiar.

Similar to the spillover effect is the crossover effect. That's when one person's emotions or attitudes "crossover" and affect another person. It's not something most of us think about, and is a bit more complicated than the spillover scenario. It refers to what happens when you have a bad day at work, come home, and *your spouse* kicks the dog.

Work and family are the two major domains in most people's lives, but many people think when they go home, they just "leave work at the office." Others watch the final minutes pass just before 5:00 PM, tick tock tick tock, until their official workday ends. But your job cannot be isolated within a defined time slot, separate from the rest of your life. Even if you leave the paperwork on your desk and silence your mobile phone at night, you and your job are still together in surprising ways. Let's take a closer look at spillover and crossover. . . .

Your Job and Your Marriage

In 1989, in northern Iowa, 337 families agreed to take part in a unique study. Reaching far beyond a simple survey or a single experiment, the families agreed to be watched and evaluated over a four-year period of time. Each family was visited twice a year by a field interviewer who gave them questionnaires and guided them through group exercises, which were videotaped for later review. Researchers at Iowa State University undertook this ambitious project as a way to specifically look at the spillover and crossover effect of work-family conflict, and what variables might link the two together.

Many of their conclusions supported prior research about the spillover effect, but researchers were surprised to find that "a spouse's job exerts as much influence on individual distress levels as does conflict from one's own job." In fact, the coefficient showing the relationship between the husband's work-family conflict level and his psychological state (0.276) was identical to the effect his work-family conflict level had on his wife's psychological state. This, in turn, had a negative impact on the marriage. We can see these linkages in Figure 2.1.[2]

Until the late 1990s, nobody had ever studied spillover by observing the daily, routine interactions of couples. Nicole Roberts and Robert Levenson are psychologists at UC Berkeley who decided to not only watch conversations between couples, but also monitor their biometrics to uncover what was happening on a physiological level. They chose police officers and their spouses as their subjects, given the unique stress police experience and the high rate of divorce among police marriages. In addition to completing questionnaires and daily diaries for a month, each couple reported to the Berkeley lab where Robert and Levenson wired them up and invited them to talk to each other about their

Figure 2.1 Work Conflict Correlates to Marital Distress

day. As the couples talked for 90 minutes, researchers recorded their heart rates and different physiological responses.

Roberts and Levenson found, as expected, that on-the-job stress spilled over into marital relationships and negatively affected both individuals. In fact, they found that mental job stress has a greater impact than physical exhaustion on marital inter-actions. But the physiological data collected showed precisely how this occurs. In a surprising result, their data showed that on high stress days, police officers exhibited higher cardiovascular activity, while at the same time having lower somatic, or bodily, activity. High stress workdays caused couples to be amped up on the inside, but cool and passive on the outside. Roberts and Levenson describe the physiological pattern as a "freeze" response associated with fear or defensiveness. And they warned that this freeze during marital conversations is a sign that couples are on a "trajectory toward marital distress and dissolution."[3]

A 1985 study confirmed that the inverse was just as true; better work experiences led to a better marriage. Researchers from New York University and the Families and Work Institute surveyed about 500 employees from a U.S. pharmaceutical company and found that having an "enriching job" was directly related to having stronger "marital companionship" (see Figure 2.2). They also

Figure 2.2 Positive Work Emotions Correlate to Marital Companionship

found that workers who had demanding jobs with little managerial support argued more with their spouses. In another example of the crossover effect, the family arguments experienced by the participants in the study actually weren't about time, or watching the kids, or managing the household—they were general arguments unrelated to work in any way, suggesting that work challenges made both partners more argumentative.[4]

Your Job and Your Children

Just as work can help or hurt your marriage, the same spillover and crossover principles impact your relationship with your children. Although many studies support these findings, two in particular—one focused on mothers and the other on fathers—offer insight into a specific chain of events.

Karyl MacEwen and Julian Barling at Queen's University studied 147 female hospital workers, all of whom had at least one child. They had the moms answer questions about job satisfaction, stress, mood, parenting behaviors, and a full 89 questions were used to measure the children's behaviors. Their results confirmed that work experiences impact job satisfaction and mood, which spills over and affects a mother's behavior toward her children, which affects how her child acts at school. Put simply, a mother's work-related mood crosses over to her children's behavior. Figure 2.3 is a simplified model of these linkages.[5]

Years later, a study set out to confirm these phenomena in fathers and for the first time sought an independent evaluator of

Figure 2.3 How Work Mood Crosses Over to Children's Behaviors

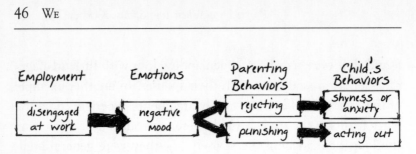

Figure 2.4 Parents' Work Moods Can Lead to Rejection and Punishment of Children

children's behaviors—namely, their teachers. This study looked at 189 dads along with their fourth- or fifth-grade children who were in 25 different classrooms. Fathers completed a questionnaire about their work experiences and mood, and teachers completed questionnaires on the students' behaviors at school. The results from this study once again confirmed that the children's behavior at school was impacted by the work environment of their fathers.

One path from their model details the factors that link job to child. It shows that workers who don't have a lot of control over their job or decision making (i.e., they perceive that they are micromanaged) have overall lower job satisfaction and this spills over into a negative mood, which they then take home with them. The more negative their mood, the more likely they are to punish or reject their children. And the more their kids are punished and rejected, the more likely they are to act out or exhibit shyness. Figure 2.4 shows a simplified version of this path.[6]

Your Job and Your Health

Does your boss have good leadership skills? Rate your boss on the following five specific indicators by completing Activity 2.4.

Activity 2.4 Your Boss as Leader

INSTRUCTIONS: Read each statement about your boss below, and indicate how often it occurs.

	Never	Seldom	Sometimes	Often
My boss gives me the information I need.	1	2	3	4
My boss is good at pushing through and carrying out changes.	1	2	3	4
My boss explains goals for our work so that I understand what they mean for my particular part of the task.	1	2	3	4
I have sufficient power in relation to my responsibilities.	1	2	3	4
I am praised by my boss if I have done something well.	1	2	3	4

Believe it or not, those five questions reveal not just the quality of your boss as a leader, but also reveal your risk of being hospitalized from heart disease (the most common cause of death in Western countries). In a 2009 study, researchers showed a direct link between managerial leadership and ischemic heart disease. They studied 3,122 men who lived near Stockholm, Sweden, and asked them to rate their bosses using a 10-question survey (the five questions above were the ones found to be most predictive). They then tracked them for the next 10 years to see which men in the study group wound up hospitalized for a heart-disease related event such as a heart attack or stroke. Using language that is typically reserved for pharmaceutical trials, the investigators noted a "dose-response relationship," in which people who rated their bosses poorly but still remained with their employer for four or more years were the most at risk. In summary, the study found that men who worked for effective leaders were about one-third to one-half as likely to be hospitalized from heart disease as those who were dissatisfied with their employers. Or, to put it another way, working for a bad boss might increase your risk of heart attack by 50 percent.[7]

In another study, six researchers in Finland wanted to see if your job could actually kill you. Of course, they probably wouldn't describe their study that way. They would say they wanted to investigate the links between certain work elements and cholesterol, body mass index (BMI), and cardiovascular mortality (i.e., death from heart attack, stroke, or other heart disease). They began the study in 1973 and surveyed 812 employees and conducted health checks after 5 and 10 years. Then they watched the participants until 2001—27 years from the start of the study—to see who of their subjects died from a cardiac event.

In results published in the esteemed *British Medical Journal*, they revealed that employees who were dissatisfied with their compensation, recognition, and career opportunities had a BMI that was 0.6 higher than those who were satisfied with their rewards. This equates to about an extra five pounds on a person of average height. More significant was the finding that workers who were dissatisfied were also 2.4 times more likely to die from a cardiac event. To put this into perspective, smoking cigarettes makes you 2 to 4 times more likely to develop heart disease. If you think smoking is harmful to your health, how about a bad job?[8]

Your Job and Your Quality of Life

After seeing how your job impacts your relationship and your health, you might assume that your job also impacts your overall quality of life. You'd be right. The link between job satisfaction and life satisfaction has been studied frequently since the mid-1950s, but with a wide range of results. It wasn't until 1989 that researchers published a meta-analysis that looked at results from 34 different studies, with a total sample size of 19,811 workers. This definitive analysis confirmed that there is a strong positive correlation between your job and life satisfaction.[9]

Keep in mind, though, that correlation doesn't necessarily mean causation. So psychologists at Cornell University set out to answer the deeper question: Did job satisfaction cause life satisfaction or was it the other way around? What other factors were at play?

Indeed, they found that the link goes both ways, but the link was stronger in the direction of job satisfaction influencing life satisfaction. As to what *drives* job satisfaction, they looked at a range of factors including hours worked, job tenure, wages paid, effort required, promotion opportunities, and working conditions. But the factors that had a substantial effect on levels of satisfaction were the intrinsic factors, such as having autonomy, utilizing one's strengths, learning new things, and having control over how to get the job done.[10]

Believe Us Now?

We've just seen how we all take on multiple roles in life, which combine to form our unique identities. Family and work are two major domains, but too often we don't realize just how important work is in shaping who we are on a day-to-day basis. Because of the psychological notions of spillover and crossover, our feelings at work impact our behaviors outside of work, thereby impacting our loved ones.

Simply put, you can't box up your job and keep it separate from the rest of your life. It doesn't work that way. Want better health? Get a job that vitalizes you. Want a passionate marriage? Get a job that you love. Want to be happy? Be truly engaged at work.

How do you get engaged at work? We'll share that soon enough. But now that we understand the importance of full engagement to the individual, let's look at how important a fully engaged workforce is to an organization.

Chapter Summary

Profits Drop When Your Spouse Kicks the Dog

(You can download this summary as a one-page PDF at www .WeTheBook.com.)

Spillover is the term psychologists use to describe when one area of your life "spills over" into another area, and *crossover* describes how your emotions and behaviors "cross over" to other people. An abundance of research shows that work factors impact your

- Health
- Marriage
- Children's behavior
- Happiness and quality of life

"Working for a bad boss may be as harmful to your heart as smoking."

Key Takeaways for Individuals

- Your identity as a worker and feelings about your job have a critical impact on all areas of your life.
- If you want a great life, you need to be fully engaged at work.

Key Takeaways for Managers

- Managers shape the work environment, which drives employee engagement, which in turn spills over into all areas of an employee's life.
- On any given day, your leadership behaviors have a far-reaching impact. You are not a doctor, and yet you have a role in your team members' health. You aren't a marriage counselor, yet you influence your team members' relationships with their spouses. You aren't a teacher, yet you contribute to how your employees' children behave in school.
- Are you living up to that responsibility?

Chapter Bonus Material

Video Interview with Rudy Karsan and Kevin Kruse

You have special access to material only available to readers of this book. Watch the interviews with authors Rudy Karsan and Kevin Kruse as they talk candidly about how their own work experiences have spilled over into other areas of their life for the better, and sometimes for the worse.

(continued)

(*continued*)

1. Go to www.WeTheBook.com
2. Click the "Bonus Material" button/link
3. Click the link that says "Spillover"
4. Enter the password "crossover" (without the quotation marks)

Enjoy your bonus material!

Part Two

The You in We

When unlocking the secret to an engaged workforce, many people assume that an organization owns the single key—that it's up to leadership to find and turn the key. Many ask, "What can Eva do to better engage the workers at her location?" or, "Acme needs to address their issues around trust and transparency to get their employees better engaged." Indeed, the role of leaders is essential.

But the *We* approach to full engagement acknowledges equally the critical role of the worker—the individual. Employees' engagement levels may be limited by the fact that they just don't fit with the company culture. Or, they may be in the wrong career, or the wrong kind of company.

Quality leadership alone isn't enough to unlock engagement. You need a second key. *You* hold the second key.

Aiming for the Career-Life
Bull's-Eye

Your work is to discover your work and then with all your heart to give yourself to it.

—BUDDHA

Successful and Unsatisfied

Jason was hired right out of college to work as a writer of corporate training materials. He was an English major with a 4.0 grade point average and a penchant for skit comedy. Super bright, he quickly moved to tougher and tougher assignments and earned a series of pay raises and promotions in record time. He was well liked by all and viewed as a real star on the team.

So, Kevin, his manager, was more than a little surprised when Jason told him one morning, "I just can't write anymore. I'm sorry to let you down, but I'm resigning."

Kevin assumed that Jason was just having a really bad day, or a stressful week in a tough month. "Hey, J, why don't we just take a break, we'll restructure the work a little bit . . ."

"No, you don't understand. I've thought a lot about this. I don't like to write. I don't want this to be my job in 20 years. I love the people here, I love the company, I'm proud of our work, but it's just not the work that I like to do," was Jason's response.

Kevin was a little puzzled. "Well, what *do* you want to do?"

"I helped run a coffee shop when I was in college and I loved it. I want to go into food service."

How could someone trade in a fast track white-collar job for food service? Kevin reacted without empathy, in a knee-jerk fashion and started talking about the low pay and long hours on your feet. Jason cut him off . . .

"Kevin, I've worked in it before, I know all that stuff. I know it's hard. I'm telling you I love it. My passion is food, the preparation of food, making the restaurant better, servicing the customers. It's what I really like to do."

It was pretty hard to argue with that.

It's now 10 years later and Jason lives with his beautiful wife and two kids in New Jersey, and he's happy and engaged at work, where he manages a fantastic bakery-café.

The Three Ps: Passion, Purpose, Pay

As with Jason's story above, you can be very successful in a profession but that doesn't necessarily mean you will find it fulfilling and engaging. Many of us end up in careers not suited for us. Many follow in the footsteps of their same-sex parent, becoming a doctor, lawyer, or other professional. Others, without direction in college, take the first good paycheck to come their way and never look back. Some may know the career they desire but feel that it's out of their reach. Unlike your parents or grandparents who had to make a 40-year career decision, you likely have to make a 60-year decision, which may involve multiple careers.

To get that deep feeling of engagement in your career, you need to find the intersection—the bull's-eye—of three very important things:

1. Passion—What are you truly passionate about? What is your ultimate dream?
2. Purpose—Where do you want to serve? In what area do you want to make a contribution?
3. Pay—What can you earn a living doing? What standard of living will you choose?

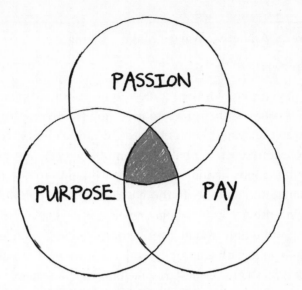

Figure 3.1   Your Career-Life Bull's-Eye

You may have several answers for each of these questions, but the Venn diagram in Figure 3.1 shows that the intersection of the answers is what you're after.

For example, you might enjoy being a coffeehouse barista, but if you are a single mom to two kids, you might not be able to pay your bills with that career choice. You might be passionate about writing poetry and want to influence other aspiring poets, but if being a poet can't support you financially, then poetry should probably be left as a hobby rather than a career. On the other hand, if your passion is poetry and you enjoy working with children, then—depending on your financial needs—maybe you can become an English teacher or poetry professor.

The notion of using passion, purpose, and pay to guide your career—the three Ps—crystallized when Rudy was talking with his friend, Gavin Kerr, about his own circuitous career path.

A Pretty Addictive Way to Make a Living

Gavin Kerr

Many people are surprised to hear of my nontraditional, circuitous career path. I'm a seminary graduate who served for a year in the Peace Corps, but later became a C-level corporate executive before finally becoming the president of the nonprofit Inglis Foundation, where we help provide independence and mobility to those with physical disabilities.

One thing I know about myself is that I love helping organizations turn around. I've always rooted for the underdog and as a young athlete, I relished joining teams that nobody thought had a chance and then helping to make them a winning team. I have great memories and pride from my first such success story, which was coaching the St. Mary's College Lacrosse team. Professionally, I was involved in the University of Pennsylvania Health System when Penn was going through some tough times and I was part of the turnaround team. Then, I was at the Mercy Health System as CEO and led their turnaround. Turnarounds are like puzzles—they're tough problems that have complicated solutions. They're stressful but fun.

When I was the COO of the Children's Hospital of Philadelphia, my son, Ryan, developed cancer and as he got more ill, he used a wheelchair a great deal. I saw the challenges he faced. I saw how he became invisible to many people, who would ask me what he wanted when he was sitting right there. Ryan has since passed away and he taught us a lot. I realized that there are a lot of people like Ryan, who have very healthy minds, but their bodies fail them. It was during this time that I decided to reconnect with my desire to serve, and I chose to focus my energy toward serving people living with disabilities—a mission that had become so personal to me.

When I joined the Inglis Foundation, many people thought I was crazy to give up a C-level paycheck from world class Children's Hospital. It's true I took a huge pay cut, but what I gave up in cash I have made up in tremendous personal rewards. We were founded in 1877, but it feels like a 133-year-old startup. I work 14 to 15 hours a day, but it is work I love to do. At the end of every day you know that what you did made a difference in somebody's life. And that's a pretty addictive career.

To learn more about the Inglis Foundation or to make a donation, visit www.Inglis.org.

Discovering your Career-Life Bull's-Eye is hard work for most and takes a lot of introspection. In fact, it might take years to truly discover it, and it may even change over time.

Discover Passion in Your Biggest Dreams

Jim Collins and Jerry Porras, in their book *Built to Last*, explain that the best companies don't just have a goal or an objective. Rather, they have a big, bold, long-term mission, which Collins and Porras call a "big hairy audacious goal" or BHAG (pronounced bee-hag).[1] Unlike simple goals, the audacity of a BHAG will make many believe it is unattainable, but the same audacity will make it motivating and energizing for those who pursue it. Great leaders have practiced this long before the term BHAG became popularized. For example, Henry Ford famously proclaimed in 1907 that he would democratize the automobile so everyone could own one. It is, of course, easier to be engaged at work if you know that you are working for a great cause.

Rudy Discovers His BHAG

Rudy gazed up at the nighttime sky in awe. He was about to discover his life goal. It was an unlikely timing for such a discovery, given that Rudy was only nine years old as he stood in a grassy field, on Mombasa Island in Kenya. And of course, he didn't realize at the time that it would become his BHAG; the term itself wouldn't be invented for another 40 years. But there he stood, beside his father and his teacher, with great anticipation.

Rudy had never even looked through binoculars before, so it was with great excitement that he took the telescope from his teacher's hands. First he looked at the moon. Then his teacher pointed out Mars in the nighttime sky, and Rudy peered through the telescope in utter amazement. He stood motionless as he gazed at the planet for what seemed like hours, oblivious to the bugs that were biting at his feet. He decided then and there, that one day he would walk on Mars.

Rudy would grow to become a man and in his 20s would immigrate to the United States with the hopes of becoming an astronaut. He discovered that he was already too old to realistically pursue professional astronaut training. With that path blocked, he pursued entrepreneurship partly because he wanted to accumulate the financial resources to one day buy a ticket for space travel. His BHAG has been an important guide in his activities and relationships. He supports politicians who are strong supporters of NASA. He made a special trip to Cape Canaveral to watch the launch of a space shuttle. And his most prized possession—in fact, the only material object that has any value to him—is one of his business cards that space shuttle astronaut Marsha Ivins took up to space with her and brought back to him as a souvenir. The card, now framed, is displayed on his office wall.

Now in his 50s, Rudy knows that actually walking on Mars in this lifetime is unlikely. His BHAG has bumped into the reality of technical constraints; there is no ship he can take to Mars and the first manned expedition is scheduled to happen around the year 2035. Yet, he has no regrets and no misgivings; he still thinks of Mars on most days. He knows that the power of a BHAG, and the reward of having a personal BHAG, comes from the journey taken and not in the fulfillment of the goal itself. (And who knows what the future may hold; after all, John Glenn ventured back into space when he was approaching age 80.)

Just as BHAGs have a power to focus, energize, and motivate an organization, a *personal* BHAG can do the same for your life and career. Your personal BHAG should be rooted in something about which you are truly passionate.

For some people, like Rudy, they discover their true passion early and craft a related BHAG effortlessly. For the rest of us, developing a personal BHAG is a longer process that can take days or even years of reflection. The first step is the hardest, but BHAGs begin when we identify our biggest dream, which will reflect our deepest passion. For some, having a "dream" or being

---

A BHAG . . . will have perhaps only a 50% to 70% probability of success.

—Jim Collins and Jerry Porras[2]

a "dreamer" has negative connotations. In fact, many are told specifically at some point—possibly from those closest to them such as their parents, spouses, or counselors—to stop chasing dreams, or that it's time to live in the real world. So it can be difficult to truly let go of our inhibitions, quiet those voices, and get in touch with our dreams. In many cases, it isn't so much figuring out what your dreams are, but to *remember what they were*. Let's begin . . .

Find a time and place where you can relax uninterrupted, and clear your mind. Think about, and write down, the things that are most important to you. If you come up with things like family, friends, or faith, try again. It's not that these aren't important in your life, but they aren't the big, motivating, secret dream we're talking about. Ask yourself these questions:

- What did you dream of becoming when you were a child?
- What are the things that make you feel energized, that give you a spark, and that makes you lose track of time?
- What topics do you talk about with such enthusiasm that it is infectious to others?
- What do you enjoy reading about?
- What would you do, if you knew you could not fail?

Recognize that your dream is *your* dream—it can take many forms. Your dream may relate to a specific experience or achievement; perhaps you want to win an Oscar. Your dream may be to be a type of person; perhaps you want to be a scientist. Your dream may be related to your environment; perhaps your dream is to live immersed in nature on a mountaintop. Your dream is your dream.

After identifying your dream, the second step is to identify the real world constraints around your dream. This is where reality intrudes—but doesn't have to squash—your dream. You may face technology constraints (e.g., the technology to travel to Mars does not yet exist). You may face relationship constraints (your responsibilities to care for your children may prevent you from traveling or taking certain physical risks). You may face financial constraints (your current debts or obligations to care for children may prevent you from investing where you need to, or may prevent you from taking an entry-level job in a new field). But just because constraints exist doesn't mean you shouldn't keep your dream. In some cases, it may just mean you need to have patience until the constraints no longer exist. In other cases, constraints just provide the road map of things you need to overcome on your journey. And even in times when the constraints make it seem unlikely that your dream will be achieved, you pursue your dream anyway, knowing the reward is in the journey itself.

Lord, grant that I may always desire more than I can accomplish.

—Michelangelo

Lastly, when it comes to personal BHAGs, you must consider carefully with whom you share it. Some goal-setting experts suggest you announce your goal to the world—to ensure your commitment, and inspire both peer support and the fear of public failure. But when it comes to a BHAG, we disagree. If you've done your dreaming homework correctly, you may have a dream that some around you won't readily accept or understand, since many people discourage lofty dreams and dreamers, with the rationale that they are doing it in your best interest. Early on, you may want to selectively share your BHAG with those whom you know will support you unconditionally. You want to nurture your BHAG so that it grows and your confidence will grow as you share it with each new person.

Rudy Shares His BHAG with Kevin for the First Time

The first time the authors met, the purpose was to discuss the possible acquisition of Kevin's company, ACI, by Kenexa. Kevin asked Rudy, the CEO, reasonable questions for this type of meeting, "So Rudy, what are your long-term goals? Where do you see growth in the future?"

Rudy answered quickly and confidently, "Well, long term I'd like Kenexa to be the first company to open an office in outer space and I'd like to walk on Mars."

Well, that's freakin' weird! It sure wasn't the "double digit growth . . . open new offices . . . become the leader . . . blah blah blah," Kevin was expecting. And although it was strange, it was also captivating. Who was this guy—Kevin's potential new boss—who thought that far into the future, who dreamed dreams that huge, who was willing to be completely vulnerable and honest in their very first meeting? Kevin appreciated his honesty and ambition. This could be fun. He started talking about his life goals, too. In fact, for the next two hours there was almost no discussion of profits, cost cutting, market analysis, or integration plans. At the end of the meeting, Kevin and Rudy quickly discussed a valuation number, shook hands, and the deal was done.

Many wonder what having a personal BHAG has to do with their professional career or being engaged at work. And does it undermine the employers BHAG? The *We* approach to goals is that simply adopting your company's BHAG alone is one-sided. Indeed, many employees may get an extra bounce in their step thinking about being a part of a company that is the leader in their industry. Others may be engaged to a degree, but might also be thinking, "Is that all there is in life? I'm going to work my butt off so one brand can overtake another brand?"

Having your own personal BHAG will serve as the North star for your path. It represents your true passion and will guide you and provide sustenance in times when you may not be fully engaged at work. You may decide to pursue your personal BHAG as part of your career choice. If your BHAG is to constantly experience nature, you could decide to become a forest ranger or ecologist, for example. If you have constraints that include providing financial resources for your children's college education, maybe you will decide to work in marketing, but for a company that focuses on an outdoor lifestyle such as REI. And still others may choose an industry that has nothing to do with the personal BHAG but offers benefits; perhaps you'll choose to teach so you can have summers off to explore the outdoors. But in any of these cases, you know how your career choice is supporting your passion.

The point is that you will actually be more engaged at work, if you realize how you are still pursuing your big hairy audacious goal or dream. All else being equal, people would rather work for a dream than for a paycheck. Discover what fuels your motivational engine, what gives you sustenance, and what makes you happy to be alive.

What Is Your Purpose?

After considering what you are truly passionate about, the second step in discovering the Career-Life Bull's-Eye is to uncover your purpose. Again and again, psychologists show us that true happiness is rare in those who don't find some way to give back. Where passion is about *what* you should do, purpose gets at *who* you want to help or *where* you want to serve. In what areas do you want to make an impact? How do you want to contribute? Use the following three activities to guide you.

Activity 3.1 The Letter

INSTRUCTIONS: Imagine you receive an envelope in the mail and open it to discover a long handwritten letter. It's from someone who is writing to thank you for all that you've done. They explain in great detail how you helped them and how you've impacted their life. Imagine the positive rush of emotions you feel as you read each sentence, knowing you have truly made a difference.

Who would you want the letter to be from? A retired senior, or maybe a child? Someone who is ill, or someone who is achieving new levels of fitness?

What do they do? Are they a soldier, or perhaps a nonprofit leader?

Is it from someone in a particular organization? Maybe it's from someone in your place of worship, or from your child's school, or local political party?

Write your thoughts in the space below.

_____

_____

_____

Activity 3.2   The Award

INSTRUCTIONS: Almost all fields offer awards for the highest levels of contribution. The Nobel committee offers Nobel Prizes in the areas of physics, chemistry, medicine, literature, and peace, among others. The U.S. Medal of Honor is the highest award given by the United States to a member of the armed forces. The Heisman Trophy is awarded to the most outstanding player in collegiate football. An Oscar is presented to top professionals each year in the film industry.

Now imagine sitting in a ballroom—in your suit, tuxedo, or evening gown—waiting for the big moment. Everyone around you has gathered in your honor. They have come to celebrate your success, your contributions to their field. Tonight is your

Activity 3.2   (continued)

night; it marks the culmination of your lifetime achievement. You feel humbled and grateful for the opportunity to have made a difference. In your dream of dreams:

Who are the people that surround you? Who has gathered to honor you?

What industry or group is honoring you?

What did you do to earn the recognition?

Use the space below to record your thoughts.

_____

_____

_____

Activity 3.3   Your Admiration

INSTRUCTIONS: Think deeply about who you most admire— they can be contemporary figures or individuals from the past. Be careful with this one. It's not who you envy—we could all browse the magazine racks in the checkout aisles and find celebrities who have fame, fortune, or abs that we wish we had. But who do you truly admire? Who do you believe is worthy of admiration?

Do you admire the artist Salvador Dali, the scientist Marie Curie, or the inventor Thomas Edison?

Do you admire one of your teachers, or your doctor?

Do you admire someone you know to be a terrific mother, or a terrific manager?

Do you admire someone you know who has written a book, or formed a group, or who runs marathons?

Use the space below to record your thoughts.

_____

_____

_____

There are, of course, no right answers; there are limitless opportunities to consider. Some will choose to make a difference directly in their place of employment, while others will choose their place of worship. Some will fight for the rights of animals, while others will choose the poor. Some will choose the arts, while others will choose science. What is *your* purpose? Where will *you* serve?

Thinking About Pay

We *need* oxygen to live, but the purpose of life is not to breathe. In this same way, an individual's earnings and a company's profits are necessary but should not be one's sole purpose. So how important is compensation? How should we think about compensation?

Can Money Buy Happiness?

Brenda Kowske, Ph.D., Kenexa Research Institute

Some say money can't buy happiness, but data from the Kenexa Research Institute shows that for those who can barely pay the monthly bills, it certainly can help—at least in terms of increasing happiness on the job. For production, warehouse, or clerical workers making less than $40,000 a year, income is positively related to employee engagement as well as to their intention to stay with an organization. While the relationship is modest, it is indeed statistically significant. However, as income rises for professional and technical workers and management, the relationship diminishes. In other words, income matters more to those making less, and for those in management, no relationship exists.

This makes sense when thinking about worker motivation theory. For years now, theorists and academicians have considered income a "hygiene factor" in employee motivation, a term referencing Frederick Herzberg's two-factor theory of motivation, published in his 1959 book, *Motivation to Work*. According to the two-factor theory, hygiene factors do not add to motivation, they can only negatively affect satisfaction if they do not reach a certain threshold. It is likely that this threshold is the point at which the individual is living comfortably. Regardless of income level, after income reaches this threshold, it can only serve as a de-motivator; if income is taken away or perceived as unfair, employees will tip the scale by underperforming, which manifests in behaviors such as not meeting goals, taking more sick days, or leaving the job.[3]

The Kenexa findings support the classic work by Richard Easterlin, who studied income and happiness levels in different countries. His conclusions, now known as the Easterlin paradox, is that money does buy happiness but only until basic needs are met. Once people have their core needs covered (e.g., food, shelter, basic health), more money has no impact on their overall life satisfaction.[4]

Money is not the most important thing in the world. Love is. Fortunately, I love money.
—Jackie Mason, comedian

So what should you take from this? First, realize that taking care of your basic needs and the needs of your family must take priority. If you are trying to uncover your Career-Life Bull's-Eye, make sure you're mindful of core expenses as you think about the *pay* part of the equation. But most people have plenty of money for their basic needs and actually fall into the trap of thinking that more material goods will lead to greater happiness, or into the trap that clawing for that next 10 percent salary bump is the way to success.

Advice on Variable Pay

If you are just entering the job market, are negotiating for a new job, or even negotiating compensation associated with a promotion, it's important to remember the increasing role of variable pay in most organizations and use it to your advantage.

First, variable pay programs offer significant opportunities. If you are a talented worker—you *are* a talented worker aren't you?—variable pay enables you to make far more money than a traditional base pay with the annual raise.

Second, if you are looking for a job or just entering the workforce you should try to pick a company that has a variable pay program in place. Regardless of how much it makes sense to the employer and employee alike, if a large organization doesn't have the systems in place to support variable pay plans, it's unlikely you'll be able to convince them of its merits on your own. A far better strategy is to ask early in the recruitment process if they have a variable pay plan and what's it like.

Third, use a two-to-one ratio when you negotiate the variable part of your compensation package. In other words, you should be willing to give up one dollar of base pay for the chance to earn two dollars of variable pay. Let's assume, for example, that you currently make $50,000 per year with no opportunity to earn a bonus. Let's also assume you want to find a new job that will increase your annual compensation by at least 10 percent, or a total monetary compensation of $55,000. If you received a job offer of $50,000 plus a potential bonus of $5,000, using the two-to-one ratio, that would be like getting the equivalent of a base salary offer of $52,500, which doesn't meet your criteria. On the other hand, if they offer a base pay of only $45,000 but a $25,000 bonus in addition, using the two-to-one ratio means the bonus is equivalent to $12,500, which, when added to the base amount of $45,000, is the equivalent of earning $57,500. This is above your target, or a good offer.

Fourth, it's not just the amount of the variable pay package but also the details of how it's comprised that matters. How much of your variable pay is tied to your individual performance, how much is tied to the team, and how much is tied to the company? How specific are the measures? What has been the track record of hitting maximum payouts in recent years?

Lastly, your bonus is a form of evaluation. Most workers are lucky to get an official review once or twice a year. Often, nonconfrontational managers offer vague feedback and write down "good" or "4" on your scorecard. But your bonus is the truest assessment of your performance and that of your team and company, if those components are included. The size of your bonus will help you to decide if you're in the right job, the right company, or even right industry.

The secret most people don't realize is that when it comes to pay, they should worry more about experiential compensation and less about financial compensation. Nonfinancial rewards have a way of providing both immediate benefits as well as experiences that can lead to further career development opportunities. Everyone is unique in terms of what they would find rewarding. You might choose to work at a given company, or in a specific position, so that you can be part of a unique team of individuals, or to be able to learn from a particular leader, or because you know you will develop new skills.

Using Kenexa as an example, team members know there are many different forms of experiential compensation, including:

- Global experience—The ability to work daily with people from all over the world, and the opportunity to actually relocate and work in one of Kenexa's 20 offices in Asia, Latin America, North America, or EMEA.
- Rapid internal career advancement—Like many mid-market-sized companies, Kenexa's growth and internal pace of change leads to many new opportunities for those who are ready to seize them.
- Schedule flexibility—The opposite of a nine-to-five culture, workers put in the hours necessary to meet client and coworker commitments but have the flexibility in their schedules to participate in family and personal interests and obligations.
- Telecommuting—Many employees work from home, enabling them to live where they want, while working for the company they want.
- Opportunity to work with the biggest brands in the world—Team members gain experience and exposure to leading organizations including nonprofits, hospitals, government organizations, and Global 5000 companies.

With engagement at work having such a dramatic impact on your life—from health, to relationships, to happiness—don't compromise on your dreams or passion to earn an extra 5 or 10 percent in pay. The real pay should include both your financial compensation and experiential compensation, which can greatly advance your salary in the long term while giving you enriching experiences and a higher quality of life in the short term.

Chapter Summary

Aim for Your Career-Life Bull's-Eye

(You can download this summary as a one-page PDF at www .WeTheBook.com)

One of the secrets to full engagement is to identify and pursue your Career-Life Bull's-Eye—a target that is comprised of the intersection of the *Three Ps*:

1. What is your passion?
2. What is your purpose?
3. What is your pay?

Key Takeaways for Individuals

In our career-lives, sometimes we pursue what we are good at or fight to join a great company, but still aren't satisfied or engaged. And it's unlikely you'll be satisfied in life if you aren't satisfied and engaged at work. Use the Three Ps process to uncover your Career-Life Bull's-Eye and use your discovery to guide you and give you sustenance, even in tough times.

(continued)

(*continued*)

Key Takeaways for Managers

Remember that you hold the key to creating an environment that will enable engagement to flourish. But it also takes a second key, which lies in the hands of your workers. If survey data tells you that overall, your team is highly engaged but you have one member who is disengaged, consider guiding them through the Three Ps process. Despite your culture and even their talents, it just may be that the work they are doing isn't igniting their passion, purpose, or pay needs.

Chapter Bonus Material

Rudy Karsan on Commodity Work

Rudy Karsan has personally advised dozens of top executives on how to accelerate their careers and maximize their compensation. See this exclusive video presentation to learn about the concept of commodity employees and noncommodity employees, and how trends in variable pay can be used to your advantage.

1. Go to www.WeTheBook.com
2. Click the "Bonus Material" button/link
3. Click the link that says "Commodity Employees"
4. Enter the password "pay" (without the quotation marks) Enjoy your bonus material!

Your Kind of People

The thing I have learned at IBM is that culture is everything.
—Lou Gerstner, former CEO, IBM

Culture

Like the culture of any society or group, culture is defined by a largely unspoken and sometimes even unconscious consensus about how people should think, speak, and act. It is this culture that gives organizations and teams a sense of distinctiveness; that allows people to identify with and be loyal to the organization; and that provides a climate, which, however good or bad, defines how things will be done. Components that make up any culture include repetitive patterns of observable behavior, group norms, values, habits of thinking, mental models, root metaphors, and symbols.

In the previous chapter, we shared tools that could help you to figure out what type of work you should be doing to maximize your engagement. In this chapter, you'll discover where you should be doing it, meaning in what type of organization. Most managers focus on a candidate's experience and achievements when recruiting for an open position, and candidates typically focus on compensation, benefits, or maybe work hours. Both sides relegate culture to an afterthought, or worse, maybe consider it something that will get fixed in orientation and training. The reality is that many new hires find they are square pegs trying to fit into round holes, and no amount of training will change that.

According to a July 2007 OfficeTeam Survey, in collaboration with the International Association of Administrative Professionals and HR.com, 38 percent of employees strongly agreed and 47 percent somewhat agreed that their company had lost a staff member because he or she wasn't a good fit with the company's work environment. More than 59 percent of hiring managers either strongly agreed or somewhat agreed that they had misjudged a candidate's fit for the company in the past, according to the same study.[1]

So, what exactly is company culture? What type of culture will you thrive in? What should you do if you are working in a company where you feel you do not fit with the culture? This chapter will help you answer all these questions and more.

Activity 4.1 Culture Clues	
INSTRUCTIONS: Consider each of these five well-known companies. Based on what you have heard/read about them, try and describe what you think their culture might be like.	
Company	**Descriptors**
Google Nike Hallmark Apple Starbucks	

The Twelve Archetypes of Organizational Culture

Okay, so what *is* company culture, anyway? Some company cultures are easier to classify than others. The classic example is to contrast IBM and Apple. Both IT companies, but with very different cultures that you can spot a mile away. Other well-known cultures include Google, known for innovation, entrepreneurship, idea-sharing, informality, and fun, with its core values described as "being a flat organization with a collaborative environment."[2] Hewlett-Packard is a company that has worked hard to maintain its culture, known as The HP Way, which is based on respect for others, a sense of community and integrity, and innovation.

In plain language, an organization's culture is its collective personality. Just like an individual personality can be measured with a psychological assessment like DISC® or Myers-Briggs®, company culture can be measured in the same way. In fact, the Kenexa Cultural Insight™ instrument (based on the work of Dr. Carol Pearson and her associates) was designed to identify the archetypes that define the unwritten values and behavioral expectations within an organization.

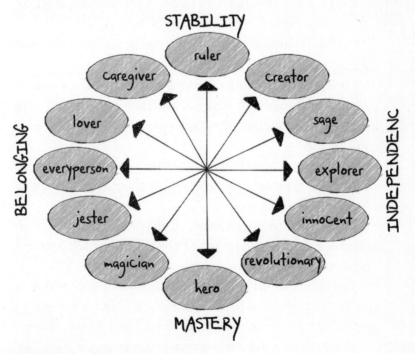

Figure 4.1 The 12 Archetypes

An archetype is a recurring personality model that appears in many places throughout history. You may recognize them as the main characters in the stories you know from fairy tales, literature, film, and the popular media. They help make knowledge that is often unconscious and unspoken, conscious and part of the articulated decision-making process for an organization and for the teams and individuals within it. These 12 archetypes reflect how much one desires independence versus belonging, and also how much one seeks stability versus mastery.

Let's take a closer look at each archetype.

Caregiver

A Caregiver organization provides service to humanity, takes care of people, and provides products and services that help others.

Values: Altruism, generosity, caring, nurturance, and compassion.

Strengths: These organizations respond to the needs of people, put people first, and put structures in place to help people and be certain they are not injured, physically or emotionally.

Weaknesses: Members of these organizations may be controlling, martyr employees, and enable client (and sometimes employee) dependency.

Brand identity examples: Campbell's Soup, AT&T, Johnson & Johnson, Mother Theresa, Princess Di, Sweden, and most hospitals and insurance companies.

You do *not* fit in: if you are self-centered or insensitive to the needs of others; are usually just looking out for yourself; or are heedless to the consequences of your actions on others.

You *do* fit in: if you feel good about helping others and feel pride in the achievements of your team and organization.

Ruler

The Ruler organization believes in power, and works to establish processes and tools that give it the support it needs to govern. The ultimate goal of the Ruler is to create the perfect system.

Values: Power, a sense of social responsibility.

Strengths: These organizations understand power, image, status, and financial affairs; and they are wonderfully able to put complex processes in place that coordinate the work of many people (and sometimes many cooperating organizations).

Weaknesses: Members of these organizations may be overly bureaucratic; elitist; slow to move; bogged down in catch-22 situations; and focused too much on internal and external politics, forgetting the needs of the customers, clients, or constituents.

Brand identity examples: The United States or any government, the Internal Revenue Service, American Express®, Great Britain, Queen Elizabeth, the Vatican, insurance agencies, regulatory bodies.

You do *not* fit in: if you don't like to follow protocol, or have problems with authority or hierarchy.

You *do* fit in: if you thrive on process, order, and accountability.

Creator

The Creator organization thrives on creative expression, imagination, and art. Creator organizations appreciate the beauty of a well-designed process as easily as the aesthetic beauty of a modern building or new luxury car. They expect that people will be happiest when using imagination to develop innovative and/or artistic products, services, and organizational structures.

The Creator organization offers people an opportunity to optimize their creativity, working individually or as part of a team effort.

Values: Imagination, beauty, new designs and forms, authentic expression, structures that are aesthetic and functional, and doing things with flair.

Strengths: These organizations can offer distinctive and custom-made products and services, often one-of-a kind. Their workplace structures may emphasize the quality of work and the way that anything becomes an art form when it is designed with style.

Weaknesses: Members of these organizations may ignore market realities, or keep creating and creating; adding on projects without letting go of any, until productive energy is crowded out.

Brand identity examples: Georgia O'Keeffe, Williams-Sonoma, the Corcoran Museum, Sony, Lucent Technologies, Crayola®, PalmPilot®.

You do *not* fit in: if you have little originality, imagination, or capacity for innovation.

You *do* fit in: if you are imaginative, creative, and enjoy working on new things.

Innocent

The Innocent organization focuses on keeping workers safe and respecting tradition. An idealist often has a vision for creating a better world. The organization typically offers products or services in a cheerful way and consistently strives to protect its customers.

Values: Loyalty, goodness, optimism, wholesomeness, allegiance to commonly held values, following established rules or principles.

Strengths: These organizations may offer a uniform product or service produced or created by employees who are not necessarily highly educated or motivated; treat employees with empathy and kindness and provide a simple, decent place to work; and are loyal to and protective of employees and customers.

Weaknesses: Members of these organizations may be resistant to innovation and have difficulty changing with the times. Such organizations may treat employees like children or control employees so that they feel like robots.

Brand identity examples: Ivory Soap, McDonald's, Walt Disney, the Pillsbury Dough Boy®, Switzerland.

You do *not* fit in: if you are overly critical, or want to innovate and go your own way.

You *do* fit in: if you are an accepting person and enjoy the security that comes from a paternalistic organization.

Sage

The Sage organization focuses on the pursuit or spread of knowledge, often from the inside out. These organizations are typically research labs, universities, and planning arms of organizations. These organizations are generally staffed by highly educated employees who demand to be treated with respect, which means they come and go as they please and are often evaluated by peers rather than by management. The working style is cool and collegial.

Values: Intelligence, objectivity, high-mindedness, dispassionate search for truth.

Strengths: These organizations are excellent at fostering an atmosphere where knowledge is advanced and passed on to the next generation. Cognitively complex, they excel at critical thinking, sound research, and in the development of methodologies to assess relative hypotheses.

Weaknesses: Sage organizations may have difficulty changing with the times or responding to market demands because employees like the freedom to do as they please. They also study problems extensively and thus often move at the speed of a glacier and have difficulty integrating cutting-edge knowledge into actual organizational practice.

Brand identity examples: Stanford University; Alan Greenspan; Japan; and most colleges, universities, and research labs.

You do *not* fit in: if you are anti-intellectual, or are not naturally curious or a problem solver.

You *do* fit in: if you are highly analytical and enjoy research and problem solving.

Explorer

The Explorer organization is outwardly focused and constantly looking for new ideas, new products, and new places to expand. It achieves growth most often through acquisition, either of new business, new products, or from external thought leaders. There are no time clocks; no one tells anyone else how to do their work as long as they are productive.

Values: Individuality, independence, self-actualization, new experiences, growth, and change.

Strengths: These organizations generally are on the forefront of theory and practice and stay current about the needs of their clients, customers, or constituencies. They provide wonderful environments for competent employees who are self-starters, allowing them to show what they can do while feeling free and unconstrained.

Weaknesses: Explorer organizations may be anarchistic, chaotic, and focused on employees, not customers or clients. They may seem to abandon employees who need more assistance. They may also lack the required cohesion to survive over time.

Brand identity examples: Starbucks; Levi's; many automobiles, especially SUVs; John F. Kennedy (especially when he said "We are going to the moon because it is there" or when he offered a cutting-edge, contemporary vision of Camelot).

You do *not* fit in: if you are a conformist or dependent.

You *do* fit in: if you stay on the cutting edge in your field and enjoy a high degree of independence.

Revolutionary

The Revolutionary organization dedicates itself to doing things differently, and breaking common tradition and practices. This type of organization does things its own way just to be unique. The Revolutionary organization has the feel of a band of committed radicals ready to overturn the status quo. Such environments tend to encourage innovation by allowing for unconventional dress, attitudes, and behaviors. Hierarchical distinctions are minimized. If you think your boss is wrong, you are expected to say so in no uncertain terms. Meetings may be a bit chaotic, and dissipative structures (ideas and events that shake things up) are encouraged.

Values: The capacity to think and act outside of ordinary boxes; a robust and energetic willingness to take risks, freedom to do and think what you please.

Strengths: These organizations recognize the limitations in ideas and thus achieve creative breakthroughs. They also undercut anachronistic, shallow, and unjust values and practices and often channel people's anger, frustration, and dissatisfaction into constructive use.

Weaknesses: Revolutionary organizations may be so anarchistic that "anything goes" and situations may fall apart; or they may engage in practices that are enough outside the mainstream or ahead of their time that investors, suppliers, customers, or the public at large lose confidence in them.

Brand identity examples: Apple, Harley-Davidson, anarchist Emma Goldman, MTV.

You do *not* fit in: if you are timid, conventional, or like the status quo.

You *do* fit in: if you consider yourself to be a nonconformist, reject traditional conservative corporate culture, and feel good being part of a cause.

Magician

The Magician organization works to help people change attitudes or trains of thought; it typically produces products that are transformational and will allow them to be more successful. The Magician culture regularly makes dreams come true. Such organizations are often vision driven and promote high individual autonomy, flexible and relatively flat structures, self-organizing teams, and an entrepreneurial spirit. They are open to turning problems into opportunities and to unexpected synchronous events that allow unprecedented success.

Values: Self-awareness, power to transform, ecological and social interdependence.

Strengths: These organizations can be high tech, high touch, high performance, and low control.

Weaknesses: Magician organizations may verge on anarchy, overwhelm employees, or expect miracles that fail to occur.

Brand identity examples: Nelson Mandela, Martin Luther King ("I have a dream"), the World Wide Web, MasterCard.

You do *not* fit in: if you are a conventional either/or thinker, cynical, or a rationalist who cannot or will not stretch to think multidimensionally.

You *do* fit in: if you want to make a difference in the world and believe that there are no limits that can't be overcome with new thinking and creative approaches.

Hero

The Hero organization admires courageous and confident people who consistently produce results. It needs a cause to champion, a challenge to overcome, or a burden to shoulder. The Hero organization tends to pattern itself after the military or a winning team in competitive sports. People are admired if they are energetic, confident, courageous, and consistently produce results. Real pride comes from striving to be the best—and sometimes achieving it.

Values: Courage, energy, focus, discipline, principled action, teamwork, "giving your all," competition, and a system that rewards people and groups in tangible ways for their superior achievements.

Strengths: These organizations are typically highly competitive, productive, and focused. They have excellent teamwork and put systems in place to fulfill their strategic objectives. They foster bravery and high performance and have great follow-through.

Weaknesses: Hero organizations often respond to stress by working harder and longer and doing more of the same, even when what may be needed is radical change. These organizations also tend to burn out employees. Teamwork can also break down, so that forward momentum is undercut by competition between team members.

Brand identity examples: Nike, March of Dimes, Germany, all military organizations, most sports teams.

You do not fit in: if you are vulnerable, laid back, or passive.

You *do* fit in: if you are competitive, achievement oriented, and thrive on a fast pace and hard work.

Lover

The Lover organization wants people to have more love or intimate friendships in their lives. The focus of this organization is inward and centers on keeping each other happy and engaged. They believe that people who love their jobs, one another, and life will do excellent work and stay motivated and loyal over time. People at all levels of the organization are close to one another, and they like to make decisions by consensus to the degree possible.

Values: Close relationships—at all levels of the organization and also with customers, clients, constituents, and suppliers; a highly developed quality of life.

Strengths: These organizations can offer a wonderful ambience and products and services that make life more pleasurable, while cementing friendship between employees, customers, suppliers, and support organizations. They excel at relationship building and creating partnerships.

Weaknesses: Lover organizations may avoid conflict; break down into cliques; get bogged down with emotional intrigue and drama; or be taken in by flattery or flatterers.

Brand identity examples: Hallmark, Victoria's Secret, Elizabeth Taylor, Cary Grant, France.

You do *not* fit in: if you put little effort into being attractive, are prudish, socially awkward, or unwilling to reveal information about your private life.

You *do* fit in: if you are relationship-driven, emotionally open, and enjoy making new friends.

Jester

The Jester organization has a playful attitude, and believes in always enjoying itself. It thinks that better results are produced when the work is fun. It is modeled on playmates enjoying themselves, clowns or comics cutting up, and inventors or entrepreneurs who maximize creativity and innovation through adopting a playful attitude that helps them tap into their cleverness. They believe that work should be fun and that when people are taking things lightly, they are smarter and better able to respond to opportunities and challenges. Flexible hours to facilitate enjoyment and innovation (such as going to the movies in the afternoon and then working all night), physical structures that help people lighten up and connect with the natural, spontaneous creativity of children (a quality many adults have lost, but one that allows openness to learning) typify this organization.

Values: Playfulness, thinking outside the box, the importance of enjoying the gift of each moment, jovial truth-telling.

Strengths: These organizations offer environments that are fun; that help people enjoy the process of responding to continuous change; that respect employee autonomy; and that invite teamwork in playful, entertaining ways that result in highly imaginative outcomes.

Weaknesses: The Jester organization may be resistant to paperwork; undervalue routine, stereotypically boring tasks; and have trouble getting down to work.

Brand identity examples: "Got Milk?" campaign, Miller Lite, Ben and Jerry's, most comics, Hawaii.

You do *not* fit in: if you are humorless, too earnest, a workaholic, or unwilling to take a joke.

You *do* fit in: if you are frequently laughing, enjoy telling and hearing jokes, and know how to balance work with recreation.

Everyperson

The Everyperson organization believes that the value of work comes from not letting one another down and finds that an environment where everyone feels they belong is most productive. Consensus building, fairness, and equality are the hallmarks of an Everyperson organization. The relationship style feels like "that old gang of mine"—a comfortable group where everyone belongs without having to be special or accomplished. Pay is not high and the physical plant is not fancy. Employees' rights are guarded and people want rules to be enforced equitably.

Values: Fairness and reciprocity ("You scratch my back, I'll scratch yours"), a sense of camaraderie based on a no-nonsense, unpretentious appreciation of people who pitch in to do their parts.

Strengths: These organizations can survive in difficult times, and they provide a sense of belonging and human dignity regardless of people's background.

Weaknesses: The Everyperson organization may be leveling; have minimal expectations of employees and customers; have inadequate quality control; and develop a culture of passive aggressiveness, griping, and protecting one's own turf.

Brand identity examples: Saturn, Wendy's, Snapple, or the bar *Cheers* of television fame.

You do *not* fit in: if you expect to be singled out for special treatment, enjoy excelling ahead of others, or desire special recognition.

You *do* fit in: if you focus on fairness and equal treatment and prefer working as a team rather than as an individual.

Knowing which archetypes are present in an organization, as well as those that are lacking, helps define an organization and helps individuals recognize the unwritten and unspoken values of the culture. To help you to see how archetype theory can be used by an organization to express its culture and employment brand, consider the case of Regeneron below.

Regeneron: The Aggressive Sage

Regeneron, a public biotechnology company, was founded with a focus on advancing science and creating an environment where scientists feel free to innovate, which they steadfastly maintained through their history. In 2007, Regeneron and one of its current partners signed an agreement to expand their collaboration, which would involve hiring several hundred new employees. There was considerable concern about the organization's ability to hire so many scientists without sacrificing quality and losing Regeneron's culture of flexibility, encouragement of innovation, and ability to move rapidly from idea to implementation. Regeneron worked with Kenexa to ensure they could articulate their culture to current and prospective employees alike.

Kenexa gathered and reviewed both qualitative and quantitative data for Regeneron. The Kenexa team spoke to more than 75 employees in all major functions at Regeneron's two major sites to gather insights and stories that revealed the emotional truths underlying Regeneron's culture. The last step was to administer the Kenexa Culture Index survey to all employees.

The strongest archetype exhibited by Regeneron was the Sage and the next most prevalent archetype was the Hero. The combination of Sage and Hero, in conjunction with the qualitative data, led to an Aggressive Sage archetypal depiction of Regeneron's culture. Building upon this archetype, senior management and Kenexa consultants expounded upon the archetype, creating The Regeneron 5—five consistent themes that represented the essence of the Regeneron culture:

- Science drives our business and passion drives our science.
- We are a select team.
- You will be challenged—every day.
- "That's the way we've always done it" is the wrong answer.
- We won't let bureaucracy block good ideas.

Once the key cultural attributes surfaced, Regeneron worked with Kenexa to develop recruiting tools and approaches to distinguish Regeneron from other competitors for talent. They used this recruiting strategy to hire the right employees *culturally* and ensured these employees possessed the technical skills and experience that would drive the necessary changes Regeneron must undergo to excel. Effectively, they could retain Regeneron's soul while changing and growing.

Before the end of 2008, Regeneron had achieved all of its aggressive hiring goals, recruiting over 350 new employees, thereby attaining over 40 percent growth in less than a year. By both objective and anecdotal measures, the quality of hires was consistent with that of existing employees and may have been higher.

Delivering Happiness: The Zappos Story

Can you imagine a company that actually offers new recruits money to quit the company if they feel they might not be able to fit into the company culture? That's how serious Zappos is about having employees live and breathe their culture. An online shoe retailer that later branched into selling other products like clothes and cookware on suggestions from customers, Zappos emphasizes the importance of culture in everything the company does.

Says Tony Hsieh, CEO, "One of the things that's really important for us, actually probably *the* most important focus for Zappos is to make sure we have the absolute best company culture and part of our culture is just having a family-like atmosphere. We just want to be about the best customer service and the best customer experience."[3] How do they achieve this?

First, their recruitment process is specifically designed to filter the recruits that will likely be a great fit in their culture. The company has 10 stated values, and interview questions assess candidates for how well they're likely to be able to fit into the Zappos world. Interviews include questions like "how weird are you?" and "how lucky are you?" But that's not all. Once people are hired, they begin a four-week-long deep-immersion program, learning about the company's high energy culture and values, at least two weeks of which involves working at their call center talking to customers. This training is compulsory, no matter what role they might have been hired to do.

A week into the program, the company offers all the trainees $2,000 to quit the company if they feel they don't fit in, along with being paid for the time they have spent working there. If any of the new recruits take them up on the offer, the company feels it is money well spent, because it is very important to them to have all employees aligned with the culture. According to Hsieh, "We offer them money to quit because we really want to make sure that people that are working at Zappos are really passionate about the company and this is the place that they want to be." Following are the 10 core values from Zappos, which are taken very seriously, and people have been fired for not living up to these values.

1. Deliver WOW through Service
2. Embrace and Drive Change
3. Create Fun and a Little Weirdness
4. Be Adventurous, Creative, and Open-Minded
5. Pursue Growth and Learning
6. Build Open and Honest Relationships with Communication
7. Build a Positive Team and Family Spirit
8. Do More with Less
9. Be Passionate and Determined
10. Be Humble

The "weirdness" aspect is basically that everyone's individuality is celebrated and employees are encouraged to have fun. Employee benefits include free food and medical coverage, and Hsieh feels that all of this, while it is initially expensive for the company, pays great dividends in the long run in terms of the level of employee engagement and performance, which extrapolates into a great experience for the customer. The extent to which customer service matters to this company is illustrated by the fact that if the shoe a customer wants is not available for some reason, they are redirected to a competitor who has it. Sounds a little extreme, but Hsieh affirms that it is this very service that assures them unswerving customer loyalty and word-of-mouth business.

"The thing we realized this year that sort of ties everything together is that customer service is about making customers happy, and the culture is about making employees happy," Hsieh says. "So, really, we're about trying to deliver happiness, whether it's to customers or employees, and we apply that same philosophy to vendors as well."[4]

Discover Your Preferred Culture

To find a culture match, start by identifying what kind of culture you like working in. This is about you, not an organization. Do you thrive in a hard-driving Hero environment, or perhaps a more thoughtful Sage environment? Are you looking for fellow radical Revolutionaries to overthrow the status quo? Take the online Kenexa Individual Archetype Profile to discover your personal archetype.

Activity 4.2   Kenexa Individual Archetype Profile

Complete this 10-minute online assessment to uncover your preferred archetypes.

1. Go to www.WeTheBook.com
2. Click the button/link that says "Bonus Material"
3. Click the button/link that says "Kenexa Individual Archetype Profile"
4. Enter the password "hero" (without the quotes)
5. Complete the assessment

Identify Your Employer's Culture

Once you understand the archetype of the organization in which you'd like to work, you need to think about the archetype of the company you're currently at, or the organization you're thinking of joining. The collective personality of an organization is comprised primarily of the personalities of the leadership—both top executives and front-line managers. Observe an organization's leaders and see how they communicate and interact. Have they gotten to know you personally, maybe exhibiting signs of a Caregiver? Are they intellectual and perhaps emotionally distant, perhaps signs of a Sage? In the dog eat dog business world, many company executives display Hero traits. Are your leaders highly competitive, driven, and maybe at risk of burnout?

If you're thinking about joining a company and aren't yet on the inside, uncovering their organizational personality can be much tougher. Always start with the recruitment materials and career page on their Web site; great companies will be crystal clear about their culture and employment brand. But don't just take their word for it! Use your professional and social networks to get insight. Google the company name and take a look at what people have to say about the company.

When you go in for an interview, soak up the culture while you're there. Are their offices painted in neutral colors and filled with cubicles, or vibrant colors with couches, beanbags, and open space? What is the dress code—jeans, slacks, or suits? How are people talking with one another—is their body language reserved or are they loud and animated? Ask specifically about the company culture.

- "How would you describe your company culture?"
- "What are your most successful employees like?"
- "How do you handle conflict?"
- "How are employees rewarded and recognized for accomplishments?"
- "What are the opportunities for growth?"

Andrea's Story

The day I finally decided to leave the insurance company I was working at was the day my boss drew a sandbox on the whiteboard with a stick figure inside. He told me I was that figure and I should not attempt to move out of the boundaries of that sandbox.

I had joined the company five years earlier, and soon realized that out-of-the-box thinking was not encouraged. Being a creative person, I felt caged at the thought of always having to stick to certain limits. I was a marketing analyst at the time and I had a passion for designing. This was a time right before desktop publishing really took off, and our company was spending tens of thousands of dollars on advertising firms. I saw an opportunity where I could take some desktop publishing classes and use this training to develop myself and use my passion to help the company.

I suggested that I could start an "in-house agency" and we could design our own materials in-house and save a ton of money. Well, my boss shot that idea down and told me there would never be a design position offered in that department. Well, despite what he said, I pursued my passion on my own. Paying for classes myself, I started creating materials at work and dabbling with different programs to help the agents. I was getting some amazing feedback from the agents in the field.

My boss soon had enough of this. I wasn't doing just my job—I was doing more. He decided to put a stop to that, and called me in for the sandbox conversation. That was the day it became crystal clear. I was passionate about what I did and

(*continued*)

(*continued*)

I enjoyed the company, but the cultural mismatch could not be overcome and I started looking for another job. Today, I work in a company where instead of staying in a sandbox, I'm encouraged to break out and go above and beyond. I am now both happy and engaged at work.

You Don't Fit. Now What?

In Andrea's story, she realized that she could never be truly happy working within the company's dominant archetype. Does this mean you leave an organization just because you don't fit its culture? Not necessarily. You may be able to find subcultures within your organization, based on the department or even the individual leader. While organizations do have a dominant culture, you might find, for example, that the production area has a Ruler culture, while the marketing department has strong Explorer-related traits. Only you can decide if the mismatch is just too great to stay. But for many, understanding their own personality and the archetype of their employer gives them the tools they need to adapt and thrive.

For example, you may have a Caregiver personality but be working in a Hero organization. This means that many in leadership will be leading through intense focus, long hours, and feelings of intense competition. These are exactly the kind of people who could use a Caregiver to prevent them from tripping over the line of productivity into burnout. Similarly, you may be a Ruler in a Revolutionary organization. You could look for ways to add organization and accountability into a passionate but sometimes disorganized style.

The power of knowing your style and the culture of your employer is that it gives you a model to work in and language to navigate with. A perfect match will certainly be a factor in full engagement; only you can decide if the mismatch can work to you and your company's advantage or needs to be addressed.

Chapter Summary

Your Kind of People

(You can download this summary as a one-page PDF at www .WeTheBook.com)

Cultural fit is an important factor that is often sidelined or ignored equally by hiring organizations and by job seekers. You can use 12 classic, familiar archetypes to identify and discuss the personality of your organization.

Key Takeaways for Individuals

- Your alignment with your company's culture impacts the quality of your work and interactions with customers.
- Complete the online Kenexa Individual Archetype Profile to discover the cultural archetype you're most comfortable with.
- You can assess a company's culture *before you join* to see how well you'll fit in.

Key Takeaways for Managers

- Know that culture counts a lot in terms of both individual performance and retention.

(*continued*)

(*continued*)

- Convey your team's culture to prospective employees and make sure to probe for fit.

If you have valued team members who don't fit the team culture, help them to understand the values of the organization and how their unique personality can support the weaknesses of the organizational personality.

Chapter Bonus Material

Archetype Quick Reference Chart

You have special access to material only available to readers of this book. Realizing your own personality archetype and remembering the strengths and weaknesses of others will be vital to your personal and professional success. Download this one-sheet summary of the archetypes and their characteristics. Keep it on your desk as a handy reminder as well as to strike up great conversations with your colleagues.

1. Go to www.WeTheBook.com
2. Click the "Bonus Material" button/link
3. Click the link that says "Kenexa Archetypes Quick Reference"
4. Enter the password "hero" (without the quotation marks)

Enjoy your bonus material!

Do What Companies Do

*Destiny is not a matter of chance. It is a matter of choice: It is not
to be waited for; it is a thing to be achieved.*

—Williams Jennings Bryan

The CEO of Your Career

Look at this list of powerful names: Wal-Mart, Exxon Mobile, Chevron, Jessica, General Electric, AT&T, Michael. . . . Wait, what? Did a couple of those names jump out at you? No, Jessica and Michael aren't actually two of America's largest corporations. But don't be shocked to see the names of individuals alongside company names. Although it may not seem obvious at first, you have a lot in common with today's companies, whether they are global giants or fast-growing start-ups. Whether you know it or not, Table 5.1 includes you; even if you are employed at a company, you are also in business for yourself.

Table 5.1 Similarities Between Corporations and Individuals

Companies . . .	You . . .
. . . choose which markets and geography to operate in.	. . . choose which industry and geography to work in.
. . . find customers who will pay for their products or services.	. . . find an organization that will pay for your services.
. . . want to grow revenues and profits each year.	. . . want to grow your paycheck each year.
. . . compete against other companies, some of which are in emerging countries that offer lower prices.	. . . compete against other workers, some of whom are in emerging countries that offer lower wages.

You will not be engaged at work if you allow your career to drift aimlessly, rather than charting a career course. You must be mindful and intentional in your career choices. CEOs actively design and implement strategies for their companies each day. Among the most critical, as they can be applied to an individual career, CEOs:

- Enlist the support of an outside board of directors
- Invest in research and development
- Market solutions aggressively
- Think globally

Like a successful CEO, you need to work on your career, and actively lead your professional efforts with intention.

Personal Career Board

Throughout history, family and faith have been among people's top priorities in life. With each, there have been shepherds to guide us—our parents teach us about family and relationships and our Imams, Rabbis, Ministers, and Priests guide us in our faith. But now that career has become so much more complicated and critical in our lives, who are our shepherds for this life domain?

CEOs of major organizations have the advantage of reporting to a board of directors. These corporate boards are responsible for a variety of things, but typically offer advice on major issues, help develop new strategies, use their considerable connections for recruiting or partnership purposes, and generally holds the CEOs feet to the fire. If the world's most successful executives can benefit from a team of advisors—including Larry Ellison of Oracle, Bill Weldon of Johnson & Johnson, Sam Palmisano of IBM, Rupert Murdoch of News Corp.—don't you think you could benefit from having a team of advisors?

A personal career board differs from your traditional advisors. It's important that you have a good lawyer and financial advisor, maybe even a banker and accountant, and that your relationship is strong with all these advisors. But those advisors are providing their advice for a fee, which by its very nature changes the relationship; in some cases it means their interest may be different than yours, and in all cases their counsel ends when payment ends. Your personal board members support you because they care about you and want you to succeed. They can give advice and speak frankly without regard to their own financial impact or whether or not you like what they have to say; their only reward comes from the satisfaction of having helped another.

So how do you build your personal career board? To identify who should be on your personal career board, complete Activity 5.1.

Activity 5.1   Your Personal Career Board

INSTRUCTIONS: (Step 1) Take a deep breath and clear your mind. Think about all the people who have loved, cared for, or invested in you in the last five years and write their names in the space below. Think about anybody who you've turned to for guidance or professional advice and write all the names in the space below. Who has given you feedback that was hard to hear, but made you better? Write these names below.

_____

_____

_____

INSTRUCTIONS: (Step 2) Now, cross out any of the names on your list who are no longer living or who are famous public figures. If any of the remaining names are of people who are now too old or in poor health or in some other way no longer able to support you, remove their names as well. The remaining names are the ones that should form your first career board.

When it comes time to ask people to join your board, just call them up if you already know them well, or send them a brief e-mail that explains your purpose and asks to schedule a phone call to discuss. Let them know you value them and have always appreciated their support (e.g., "Your advice has always been valuable. . . . Your experience and insights into this industry are substantial. . . .") and that you'd like to get their advice on a more routine basis. Be clear that this role won't take too much of their time, but you'd love to be able to chat with them on the phone or via e-mail each month and meet as a group once a quarter.

Asking Complete Strangers for Advice

Think big when recruiting your career board. Even if you don't have a strong relationship with someone, he might be willing to help you out. A case in point, Kevin started his second business, a corporate training company, at the ripe old age of 25 (after his first company crashed and burned after only 12 months in business). At the time, there was a company in the Boston area that focused on the same industry niche Kevin was pursuing. The business was well-known and considered the 800-pound gorilla in its space. That company had been started years earlier by a young woman named Carol, who was legendary for her business exploits.

Everybody in the industry knew Carol. Everybody, that is, except for Kevin, who desperately wanted to learn the secrets to her success. At a time before e-mail was common, Kevin knew he had to cold call Carol if he hoped to get one or two pearls of wisdom. He dialed the phone nervously and asked the receptionist to speak to her. He expected to be put through to an assistant or perhaps to voice mail. To his surprise:

"Hello, this is Carol," she answered brightly.

"Uhhhhhh . . . Hi, Carol, my name is Kevin Kruse. Um, I know you don't know me, but I just started a company—literally three days ago I started a company—and my dream is for it to become as big as your company one day. We're sort of in the same business, but of course, I have one employee and you have 100. I was just hoping I could pick your brain and get some advice . . ."

Without hesitation, she answered, "Sure. Why don't you come up next week and spend the day with us? I'll show you how we do things up here and introduce you to everybody."

It was that simple.

A week later, Kevin was in Boston soaking up lessons that would serve him well for years to come. Within a year of the initial meeting, he and Carol would partner on client projects together and many of the people he met in Boston remain friends to this day.

You should have a set schedule for when you meet with your career board, just as CEOs have a set schedule with their boards. You can of course call upon individual members as needed, but get in the habit of sending your board an e-mail update at least once a month. It can be a simple message letting them know of your progress against goals, any issues you are struggling with, and things you've done to expand your knowledge and skills. Once a quarter, you should gather your board for a meeting, ideally face-to-face. You can pick up the tab at a nice restaurant or invite people to chat over drinks. These quarterly meetings will be the best ways to get the group brainstorming on your behalf.

Like most things in life, the more effort you put into your career board the more you'll get out of it. While not every meeting will yield a breakthrough, your board will be there for you during the more difficult times of your life and will help you seize opportunities as they arise. Perhaps most importantly, your board will hold you accountable. No longer will you just float by, letting weeks turn into months and months into years before you notice where you career has drifted. You will become mindful of your career, your goals, and what you need to do to achieve them.

Personal R&D and Learning

Companies realize that they must constantly improve their product and service offerings if they want to survive as a company. Pharmaceutical companies invest in research and development (R&D) to launch new drugs, software companies invest to add new features to their programs, automotive companies invest to make their cars safer and to update their aesthetic designs—the list goes on and on. Put another way, customers give companies money in exchange for some value, and if the company doesn't change and improve, the changing market will make their solutions obsolete or competitors who are improving will begin to offer more value for the same amount of money. CEOs believe this three-word axiom to be self-evident: change or die.

For large companies, investments in R&D can range anywhere from 3 to 9 percent of their annual sales depending on their industry, the size of the company, and what country they are in. North American companies spend approximately 5 percent of sales on R&D.

How much do you spend each year on your personal research and development and learning? What do you spend on school tuition, seminars, training programs, nonfiction books, or other professional development activities? Do you spend anything?

If you want to do what companies do and invest 5 percent of your annual income into your personal R&D, that means:

- If you earn $25,000 a year, you should spend $1,250 on personal R&D.
- If you earn $50,000 a year, you should spend $2,500 on personal R&D.
- If you earn $100,000 a year, you should spend $5,000 on personal R&D.

That's a lot of money, isn't it? Does it seem like a worthwhile investment? Imagine, though, that you are pouring that much money into your growth and development each year. It sure would give you an edge in keeping your current job, getting a promotion, or jumpstarting a move into a new industry.

In fact, an investment in education alone can have a massive impact on your career and lifetime earnings (see Figure 5.1). According to the U.S. Bureau of Labor Statistics, a college graduate earns, on average, $20,000 more than someone with just a high school education. Already have your bachelor's degree? Earn an extra $10,000 each year if you have a master's degree.

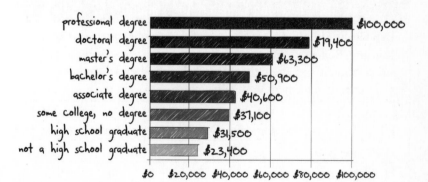

Figure 5.1 Average Annual Income by Degree Obtained

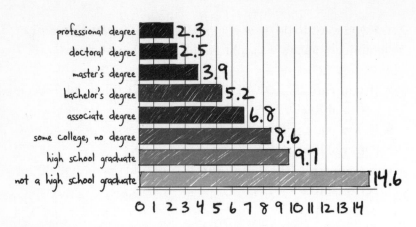

Figure 5.2 Unemployment Rate by Education Level (in 2009)

And education doesn't just drive earnings; it reduces risk to your career. Figure 5.2 shows the relationship between education and unemployment for 2009, and reveals that your risk drops almost by two-thirds if you have a college degree.[1]

But this isn't just about academic credentials, and your personal R&D doesn't require spending a lot of money. Most important is your own mind-set and intrinsic motivation to learn. Are you already a lifelong learner? Complete Activity 5.2 to find out.

Activity 5.2   Lifelong Learner Assessment

INSTRUCTIONS: Consider each of these eight statements about learning. Reflect on how much you agree with the sentiment of the statement and circle the number that most closely matches your level of agreement or disagreement.

	Strongly Disagree	Disagree	Neutral	Agree	Strongly Agree
Learning is fun.	1	2	3	4	5
I always want to grow as a person.	1	2	3	4	5

Activity 5.2   Lifelong Learner Assessment (continued)

	Strongly Disagree	Disagree	Neutral	Agree	Strongly Agree
There are many different ways to learn something.	1	2	3	4	5
In the past I've learned a lot on my own.	1	2	3	4	5
I'm a quick learner.	1	2	3	4	5
I could list many things I'd like to learn about in the future.	1	2	3	4	5
I enjoy the challenge of trying to learn a new topic or skill.	1	2	3	4	5
If I can't understand something right away I'll take a different approach to learn it.	1	2	3	4	5

Calculate Your Total Score
Instructions: Simply add up all the numbers you circled = _____

Educational psychologists have developed many different assessments that measure a person's affinity for learning. The assessment in Activity 5.2 is designed to measure the four major dimensions of your motivation to learn: a love of learning, confidence in your ability to learn, self-identity as a learner, and comfort level with challenging learning assignments. If you scored 32 or higher, you already have a high degree of self-motivation when it comes to lifelong learning. Anything less and you should consider developing your attitudes toward learning further. You may want to talk to the most successful people you know and ask them about their own habits when it comes to continuous learning. Realize that there are many ways to learn; if you are bored by reading or don't like studying alone, perhaps you should try live seminars or workshops.

An individual's career, just like a business, will perish if he or she doesn't continuously invest in new knowledge and skills. You should go to work each day knowing that you face competition from colleagues on the other side of the cubicle wall as well as from strangers in distant lands. If your employer can hire someone to do your job better than you, and at a cheaper price, eventually they will.

Your Message, Your Reach

Go Google yourself. You know, type your name into Google or one of the other major Internet search engines and see what comes up. We'll wait. . . .

Did you really do it? The results of your search are basically what your brand is to those who don't already know you. And if you didn't actually show up on page one or two of Google, that means you have no brand to speak of. The idea of personal branding is in vogue, but one's reputation and relationships have always been crucial to career success. Today is no different. What you do, and what you write, still defines you. With the Internet, it's just easier than ever before for your brand to be discovered and followed.

What you have to realize is that whether you want to be on Google or not doesn't matter; you're already there. Google indexes hundreds of millions of Web pages including the sites of local newspapers, associations, and social media sites. If you were ever arrested for driving under the influence (DUI) or had a court appearance, Google probably knows about it. If you run in 10K races or marathons that use an electronic scoreboard, Google knows your times. If you wrote a politically incorrect humorous blog post as a college student, although it might not seem so funny anymore, Google probably still has it. If you've ever donated to a political candidate or signed an online petition, yes, Google will tell the world what your political leanings are. And beyond Google, you can be sure that as you apply for new jobs or go for that big promotion, savvy HR professionals and hiring managers aren't just looking you up on Google; they are also checking you out on Facebook, LinkedIn, MySpace, Twitter, and any other place they can think of. So what do you want them to see when they find you? Do you want your brand to be regular-guy-who-drinks-beer-and-watches-football or maybe even born-again-Christian-Republican-member-of-the-NRA? There's nothing wrong with either of those profiles, of course, but will they help you to advance your career?

Rather than your brand being unintentionally defined by your personal activities, it is far better to intentionally build your brand in a way that makes people conclude, "Wow, he's really connected in the industry and knows a lot about our space." At the risk of oversimplification, do things and write about stuff that you want to be known for. If you want to be known as an innovative marketer, write about innovative marketing tactics. If you want to be known as a great Ruby on Rails programmer, moderate a message board dedicated to Ruby on Rails. If you want to be known as a leader in human resources, organize a local HR conference. With the ease of online publishing and the insatiable appetite associations have for volunteers, there are unlimited opportunities to build a reputation among your peers that can be found through Google.

Half of personal marketing is about what you're known for— your brand—but the other half is about *reach*. How many people do you know, and how many people know you? Gone are the days of stodgy business card exchanges and contrived meet and greets. From keeping in touch with former colleagues to staying in touch with current prospects, Internet technologies and social media platforms have reduced the friction of making and keeping connections. Now, although people can connect with you on LinkedIn, subscribe to your blog posts through RSS feeds, and follow your posts on Twitter, you don't need to jump on every shiny new Web platform. In fact, the traditional ways to keep in touch—handwritten thank-you cards, phone calls to say hi, dinner parties, and holiday cards—are increasingly rare and thus valuable in a high-tech world.

Level Five Relationships

We all have many types of relationships with varying degrees of closeness. We may have a best friend who we would literally give our lives for, people we may know but don't have a true relationship with, and everything in between. Activity 5.3—the Kenexa Relationship Rubric (KRR)—was developed as a means to evaluate and track the impact of close business relationships between Kenexa and its clients. Using the KRR scale, a Level 5 relationship represents your closest friends and colleagues, Level 0 represents your weakest relationships, and Levels 1 through 4 are somewhere in between. Pick a person who you think you have a strong professional relationship with and complete Activity 5.3 to see if they are truly a Level 5.

Rudy makes it a habit to develop at least one new Level 5 relationship each year, and currently has over 25 such connections.

Activity 5.3   The Kenexa Relationship Rubric

INSTRUCTIONS: This 10-item evaluation was validated with internal research and was found to be highly predictive of contract renewals and business growth. To evaluate a particular relationship with a client or other person, answer these questions.

1. This individual returns my calls within 24 hours.	Yes	No
2. In the last 24 months one of us has granted the other a personal favor.	Yes	No
3. In the last 12 months we have spent one continuous hour talking about nonbusiness related items.	Yes	No
4. In the last 24 months we have spent four hours in continuous presence of each other with less than six people present.	Yes	No
5. In the last 12 months we have spoken at least 12 times with one another.	Yes	No
6. I know the number of members of his/her immediate family, including most names.	Yes	No
7. In the last 12 months we have had a long meal together with less than six people present.	Yes	No
8. In the last 24 months we have discussed a major personal issue.	Yes	No
9. We have had a disagreement and it did not materially affect our relationship. (If the answer to the first half of the question is no, then the entire answer to the question is no.)	Yes	No
10. We have called each other at least once in the last 12 months just to say "hi."	Yes	No

Calculate Your Total Score

INSTRUCTIONS:

1) Add up all the numbers you circled = _____.

2) Divide the number of yes's from step one by two = _____.

3) Round up the number in step 2 if not an even number = _____.

If you answered "yes" to 9 or 10 of the questions, you have a Level 5 Relationship.

Less close, but still important to Rudy are another 600 individuals that he maintains contact with a few times a year and who are on his holiday card list. If he included more casual relationships, he has over 2,000 individuals in his contact directory.

Kevin has fewer Level 5 relationships than Rudy but many more Level 0 relationships. Over 10,000 people ask Kevin to send them his weekly e-mail newsletter, he maintains over 2,500 followers on Twitter, and accepts invitations to connect on LinkedIn from anybody who asks him to. A phenomenon known as the "strength of weak ties" shows that these types of connections, while weaker, can provide greater access to people, companies, and information than strong ties, simply because they are so much greater in number.

Both Rudy and Kevin are seen as connectors because they maintain friendships from so many diverse groups, including industry associations, nonprofits, political groups, college alumni, neighbors, and employees in their own companies. Time and again, this large network of friends has proven valuable as a source of support, information, and referrals.

Organizations carefully craft messages that support their desired brand, and send those messages out through various channels. As the CEO of your own career, you also need to think carefully about what you want to be known for and use a variety of methods to communicate and relate. Your personal R&D efforts naturally flow into your personal marketing efforts. If you spend the time and energy to be a continuous learner, simply sharing your findings or layering your own thoughts and recommendations on top of others' work will go a long way to cementing your brand as a thought leader.

Think Globally

Thomas Friedman, in his 2005 book *The World Is Flat*, showed that beyond a doubt globalization has made geographical boundaries largely irrelevant, thus increasing the competition for business and jobs. Indeed, if you look at the 500 U.S. companies that make up the S&P list, 40 percent of their combined revenue now comes from overseas. The world's largest pharmaceutical company, Pfizer, gets over half its revenue from outside the United States, and Nike is experiencing all of its growth from emerging markets like China and Russia. Most startling is the fact that in 2009, China became the world's largest market for automobiles, and General Motors now sells more cars in China than in the United States. This phenomenon extends to mid-market companies as well—even Kenexa gets 25 percent of its revenues from outside its home country.

One Expatriate's Story

Matt McKelvey

Prior to turning 25, I was a shining example of the stereotypical American with a very narrow global perspective. My language skills were limited to English and an unsuccessful two years of high school Spanish. I did not hold a passport, and with the exception of a couple Mexican and Canadian border towns, had not traveled outside the continental United States. After college graduation, I finally left my hometown of Lincoln, Nebraska, and only made it about 300 miles south to Wichita, Kansas.

In 2000, my company offered me the opportunity to spend several months in London working to expand our business there. I jumped at the opportunity and while my initial stint was for a brief six months, it was enough to discover that international assignments provide a steep learning curve, high degree of ambiguity, wide breadth of responsibility, and increased accountability. I was quickly

(continued)

(*continued*)

hooked on living in an international city and the opportunity it provided to experience diverse culture and cuisine, to travel, and to meet people from all over the world.

I returned to the United States, but shortly after the 9/11 attacks, I left again and set off for Purdue University's Krannert School of Management to get my MBA. Upon graduating, I was fortunate to receive many offers, and ultimately I chose one of the world's largest computer companies, believing that the organization would provide the best path to international opportunities. And as it turned out, while in the middle of a move to their headquarters in Texas, they offered me the chance to immediately join a start-up team for the company's new call center in Manila. My tenth day on the job, I left for Asia.

Launching a new facility in an emerging market, under a global brand, was a powerful experience. While my assignment focused on managing the staffing function related to growing the site from 5 to 2,000 employees, I also gained significant experience across all human resources functions as well as government and community relations. The cultural and economic environment of the Philippines was substantially different than anything I had ever experienced. I quickly became very fond of the country and its people. The jobs we created in Manila had a considerable impact on the country's labor market. Being a part of that growth, and seeing how it improved the quality of life of our employees and their families was tremendously rewarding.

After completing the assignment in Manila, I returned to the States and then joined an HR technology company that would have me living and working in England, Germany, and eventually Visakhapatnam (Vizag), India. The 18 months I spent living in India were the most rewarding of my life. We exceeded the expectations for growth in that office and Vizag is now the second largest location in the company. More importantly, we created additional opportunities for our employees there, improved engagement, and established a stronger sense of culture. Living in India was amazing and life in a "tier-two" city certainly provided its share of social challenges.

My latest post has me living in Shanghai, China, where I'm assisting with the integration of a newly formed joint venture while continuing my operational focus in India. I now find myself in another steep learning curve as we address product localization, service delivery, and M&A strategy for China— not to mention Mandarin classes three days each week.

Aside from the clear developmental benefits, I have accumulated some amazing life experiences: swimming with a whale shark while Scuba diving in Thailand, sailing under Tower Bridge in London (while it was opening) on my birthday, meeting the president of the Philippines, walking on the Great Wall two weeks in a row, and attending a *satsang* overlooking the Bay of Bengal in India. I have accumulated many rewarding personal and professional relationships that span the globe. While I miss my family and friends all over the world, Shanghai is home for now.

As businesses of all sizes have gone global, the demand for globally minded workers has skyrocketed as well. People who are willing to travel, to relocate, and to embrace new cultures have a distinct advantage over those who aren't. Kenexa researchers Vernon Bryce and Richard Harding studied *multi-patriates*—those who live, learn, work, and play in a huge range and rich mix of geographies, cultures, and faiths—and who achieved considerable success in their careers. After conducting a series of qualitative interviews, they found 12 universal traits common to most multi-patriates:

1. Openness—A capacity to approach people and experiences with "open arms; without prejudice."
2. Empathy—Deep, spontaneous concern for and awareness of others' needs and feelings.
3. Positivity—Immediately and habitually seeing and expressing the upside of situations and people.
4. Altruism—Natural appreciation of goodness; generous desire to contribute to the good of others.
5. Confidence—Awareness of internal strengths; also how to apply them to new challenges.
6. Flexibility—Spontaneous and seamless response to new information and new approaches.
7. Team-orientation—Preference for working in a group; effective within groups, adds to groups.
8. Work-focused—Need for work to be a central and dominant part of their life; work is their life.
9. Curiosity—Attraction to novelty and the unusual, as well as finding out how others live and do things.
10. Learner—Constant desire for new experiences from which to develop new knowledge and skills.
11. Imagination—Capacity to see beyond the now, beyond daily reality, and to visualize how things can be different.
12. Resilience—Emotional toughness under extreme new social and cultural pressures and opportunities.

Many successful multi-patriates communicate a strong desire for new experiences and an urge to keep exploring; they often express puzzlement that others did not share these needs. Do you have what it takes to be a global career warrior? Take the assessment in Activity 5.4 to find out.

Activity 5.4 The Multi-Patriate Character Fit

INSTRUCTIONS: For each of the 36 statements, circle the number that applies to you. You can also complete this exercise online with automatic scoring by going to www.WeTheBook.com.

	Low	Neutral			High
Openness					
My friends are all very different.	1	2	3	4	5
I really enjoy talking to all kinds of people.	1	2	3	4	5
People say I have friends all over the world.	1	2	3	4	5
Empathy					
The deep feelings of others affect me deeply, too.	1	2	3	4	5
It makes me sad to see or hear of others' suffering.	1	2	3	4	5
People often say I care too much about others.	1	2	3	4	5
Positivity					
The brighter side of life always attracts me.	1	2	3	4	5
I can often find the upside in the most extreme situations.	1	2	3	4	5
When traveling to far-off places I feel very excited.	1	2	3	4	5
Altruism					
I really enjoy helping other people who need me.	1	2	3	4	5
I have given my last penny to somebody who needed it.	1	2	3	4	5
The vast majority of people in this world seek goodness.	1	2	3	4	5

(*continued*)

123

	Low	Neutral			High

Confident

I am very capable when compared with others.	1	2	3	4	5
People say I seem to overcome obstacles easily.	1	2	3	4	5
When facing tough situations, I know there is a way through.	1	2	3	4	5

Flexibility

At work or traveling I can just go with the flow.	1	2	3	4	5
I love finding new ways to do new things.	1	2	3	4	5
Change always seems to energize me.	1	2	3	4	5

Team

One person can make a real difference.	1	2	3	4	5
Two minds are always greater than one.	1	2	3	4	5
I always make time to be with people.	1	2	3	4	5

Work

Work helps me to meet more people quickly.	1	2	3	4	5
Compared with other things, work is extremely important to me.	1	2	3	4	5
I find that in new places I work better than in familiar ones.	1	2	3	4	5

Curiosity

I really enjoy traveling to experience unusual situations.	1	2	3	4	5
My friends say I have always shown interest in how others live.	1	2	3	4	5
People I meet in new places often say I ask a lot of questions.	1	2	3	4	5

Activity 5.4 (continued)

	Low	Neutral			High

Learning

Every new experience teaches me something.	1	2	3	4	5
There are so many things to learn in new places, I often run out of time.	1	2	3	4	5
Wherever I go I know I will learn totally new ways of looking at things.	1	2	3	4	5

Imagination

People say I have the unusual habit of looking to the future.	1	2	3	4	5
Everywhere I go I seem to understand things more than others.	1	2	3	4	5
I'm always coming up with new ways of doing things.	1	2	3	4	5

Resilience

People say I'm emotionally pretty tough.	1	2	3	4	5
I just seem to bounce back even when I've made a mistake.	1	2	3	4	5
In new places I know I can work through any new pressures.	1	2	3	4	5

Calculate Your Total Score

INSTRUCTIONS: Simply add up all the numbers you circled = _____.

If your total score is less than 108, you probably wouldn't be comfortable as a country-hopping multi-patriate. Focus on being successful in your home country. But if your score is 108 or higher, you may want to capitalize on your penchant for new experiences and pursue work opportunities around the globe. Your adventures in the global marketplace will likely accelerate your career and lead you to ever higher levels of engagement at work.

Be Mindful

Although there are many tools for self-discovery and suggestions for how you can actively advance your career, for both financial gain and increased engagement, ultimately being the CEO of your own career is mainly about being *mindful* of your career. The CEO of a business is paid to grow that business and is held accountable by his or her board of directors. Similarly, you need to make the growth of your career a priority, be mindful of its progress, and think like a big company CEO. It's easy to be mindful of many other things day in and day out—from our kids' school activities to the playoff race of our favorite team—while just showing up and doing our job and collecting our paycheck. And if we aren't paying attention, we just might go into work one day to find out that our job, or our employer, no longer exists.

Chapter Summary

Do What Companies Do

(You can download this summary as a one-page PDF at www .WeTheBook.com)

Being engaged in your daily work goes hand in hand with being engaged and mindful of your long-term career. To maximize opportunity and minimize risk, be inspired by the actions of big company CEOs and do the following:

- Assemble a personal career board.
- Invest in personal R&D; be a lifelong learner.
- Market yourself aggressively.
- Think globally.

Key Takeaways for Individuals

Many individuals go with the flow and just assume their jobs are secure, their company is healthy, and their industry will exist forever. These are the people who are surprised when they lose their jobs, and are further surprised when they can't find another. Work hard to develop a deep understanding and self-awareness of where your strengths lie and where you will likely find success, and then actively and continuously grow your career.

Key Takeaways for Managers

Sometimes you can do everything right and your direct reports still won't be engaged. The *We* approach to workforce engagement acknowledges that the manager and the employee must work equally hard at being engaged at work. Whether you are a manager or an employee, encourage fellow team members to be mindful of their careers and support them as they plan their futures and set long-term work goals.

Chapter Bonus Material

Kevin Kruse on Social Media

When it comes to establishing and maintaining a personal brand online, it can be easy to be overcome by all the social media tools and conflicting advice out there. In this exclusive bonus, watch a recorded screen cast of Kevin Kruse providing an overview of the tools and methods he uses on a daily basis to cultivate an online brand.

1. Go to www.WeTheBook.com
2. Click the "Bonus Material" button/link
3. Click the link that says "Kruse on Social Media"
4. Enter the password "social" (without the quotation marks)

   Enjoy your bonus material!

Part Three

How Great Leaders Harmonize Teams

While being engaged at work is critical for one's life and society, it doesn't by itself translate into gains for the employer. Employees may be very engaged but not working in a way that benefits the organization, or worse, may be moving in competing directions at the same time. It is only when engaged employees are also aligned to an organization's purpose and goals that you are able to achieve what we call *harmonization*.

Harmonization =
Engagement + Alignment

Always aim for complete harmony of thought, word, and deed.
— MAHATMA GANDHI

What Is Employee Engagement?

Despite the high unemployment that accompanied the Great Recession that started in December of 2007, business leaders still stay awake at night thinking about how to hire and retain great talent. They know that the knowledge, skills, attitudes, and effort of their workers are critical to both immediate and long-term success. The ubiquitous phrase, the "War for Talent," has been used as a rallying cry that encompasses everything from recruitment to training to retention, and those things remain critical. But with leaders looking for productivity gains from every avenue and with the pressure of recruitment temporarily eased, employee engagement has become the hot priority. But what exactly *is* it?

Let's start by clarifying what employee engagement is *not*. It does not simply refer to employee satisfaction or happiness. Although satisfaction is one component of engagement, a satisfied employee might still be one who hops up from their desk at 5:00 PM sharp, or takes that head hunter phone call looking for that 5 percent bump in pay, or goes home and mumbles "fine" when asked how their day was at work.

Engagement, on the other hand, although uncommon, is something you can easily recognize when it's present. You see it in the waiter who addresses his regular customers by name. You see it in the office worker who looks up at the clock mid-afternoon and mutters to no one in particular, "Oh, I forgot about lunch." You see it in the TSA agent who actually greets you by name and with a smile and comments on the city from which you are traveling. You see it in the worker who offers up the names of three friends when she learns that there is a job opening in her company. Engaged employees are ones who routinely go the extra mile, not just so they can succeed, but also so that their organization can succeed.

Many different definitions of employee engagement have been developed and the one that most accurately describes it is the following:

> Employee engagement is the extent to which employees are motivated to contribute to organizational success and are willing to apply discretionary effort to accomplishing tasks important to the achievement of organizational goals.[1]

This definition implies that engagement is an internal emotional *state*. It's a precursor both to a higher degree of commitment and to a desire to stay in an organization. In this sense, employee engagement is not performance but rather a precondition that leads to greater performance.

Employee engagement is indeed something that can be measured. The Kenexa Employee Engagement Index is comprised of four simple but powerful statements, which employees are asked to rate on a scale from 1 to 5:

1. I am proud to work for my organization.
2. Overall, I am extremely satisfied with my organization as a place to work.

Figure 6.1 Components of Employee Engagement

3. I would gladly refer a good friend or family member to my organization for employment.
4. I rarely think about looking for a new job with another organization.

In short, employee engagement is about pride, satisfaction, advocacy, and retention, as illustrated in Figure 6.1.

So how engaged are you, right now, in your current job? To find out, answer the four engagement questions in Activity 6.1.

Activity 6.1 Your Level of Engagement

INSTRUCTIONS: Consider each of these four statements and circle the number that most closely matches your level of agreement or disagreement (from 1 = Strongly Disagree to 5 = Strongly Agree).

	Strongly Disagree	Disagree	Neutral	Agree	Strongly Agree
I am proud to work for my organization.	1	2	3	4	5

(continued)

Activity 6.1 Your Level of Engagement (continued)

	Strongly Disagree	Disagree	Neutral	Agree	Strongly Agree
Overall, I am extremely satisfied with my organization as a place to work.	1	2	3	4	5
I would gladly refer a good friend or family member to my organization for employment.	1	2	3	4	5
I rarely think about looking for a new job with another organization.	1	2	3	4	5

Calculate Your Engagement Score
Add up all the numbers you circled
Divide that total by 4 and write your score
here = _____

Measuring engagement with this instrument is typically done for a team, division, or organization, not for an individual. But you can use your individual score as one way to explore your own emotions at work. If you responded favorably to all the questions in Activity 6.1, rating each question a 4 or 5, you are considered engaged. If you chose "strongly disagree" or "disagree" for all four items, you would be considered disengaged at work. Of course, if you chose the "neutral" answers, you'd be neither engaged nor disengaged.

It's important to know that being engaged is different from being happy, and unhappy doesn't necessarily mean disengaged. Some individuals may be frequent complainers, but they may still be the most engaged people in the company—they complain because they care. Or, they may be too busy and engaged to feel like smiling or to get outwardly excited during a department celebration. In fact, you can have a deeply unhappy employee who is thoroughly engaged and aligned with your business strategy. Likewise, you can have smiling, laughing, cheerful employees who aren't aligned at all with the company's performance objectives. They're not productive. They're just having a good time.

Are You Happy Being Unhappy?

Are you unhappy at work but feel hopeless about the situation? Maybe you don't like the work or your boss, but you "need the money" or "there are no other jobs." Do you frequently complain to others about your boss and colleagues? If this doesn't sound like you, you probably know someone at work who it does sound like; someone who always seems to see the worst in his or her situation.

Unfortunately, many people have discovered a way to be happy being unhappy. Think about it—if someone is *that* unhappy, why don't they just quit and get another job? Some might like to quit their jobs but don't because they want the great benefits, or it's near the bus stop, or it offers hours that accommodates them. Well if that's the case,

(continued)

(*continued*)

then they can focus on those positive benefits (i.e., reasons why they *like* their job).

It's okay to vent after a bad day at work; we all do it. It's okay to be constructively critical. But if you find yourself always complaining to others about your work, you may need to consider what you are getting in return from it. Why do you complain about your job? Are you wearing your displeasure as a sign of superiority or to let people know that you deserve better? Are you complaining because you enjoy the sympathy and attention your friends and family give you in return?

With a slight shift in attitude you can realize that despite your difficult boss or the more tedious tasks, you can *choose* to be happy about the pay, commute, hours, or whatever keeps you there, and thereby shift your focus to the ways in which you are serving others (whether customers, colleagues, or society).

I don't worry about an employee who complains. It shows they care. I worry about an employee who stops complaining.

—Rudy Karsan

People Are People

Some people slough off the responsibility of leadership by falsely believing that their workers are immune from the power of full engagement. The naysayers may claim:

- We only employ low-skilled workers; they're fully engaged just by having a good job with good pay.

- Our country and culture is different; our people expect tough managers here.
- Our industry isn't a warm and fuzzy one; big sticks get better results than carrots.

It is true that *levels* of engagement do vary widely from country to country. Work from the Kenexa Research Institute shows that among 14 countries studied, workers in India are the most engaged and the engagement score for India is twice that of the lowest ranked country, Japan. It is also true that engagement levels vary by industry, with high-tech manufacturing ranking the highest and government workers ranking the lowest.[2]

Yet, the Kenexa surveys of over 10 million people per year in more than 150 countries in a variety of industries indicate that the engagement naysayers are wrong. In fact, all over the world, people are people. While levels of engagement vary greatly, the fundamental drivers—those things that lead to feelings of engagement at work, the things that make us say *We* when we describe our employer company—are largely universal, regardless of your country, industry, or occupation.

Based on our survey research and our own real-world experience as leaders of highly engaged teams, we have identified growth, recognition, and trust as the top three factors that drive engagement. Slightly less universal, but still consistently prevalent are teamwork, communication, future vision, corporate responsibility, and product or service quality as drivers of engagement. These are the things we all crave. These are the things that, when present, instill emotions that lead us to feeling fully engaged in our work.

There are indeed differences in the way these drivers are actualized from country to country and person to person. How an employee develops a feeling of trust in their CEO may be different in Russia than it is in Brazil. But you wouldn't find a worker in either country that would prefer to distrust their CEO. The way you might effectively listen and communicate with workers in China may be different than ones in Canada, but you won't find workers who prefer to be ignored. Around the world it would be difficult to find someone who didn't want to grow, be recognized for achievements, and have a sense of trust and confidence in their leadership. People are people.

Engagement Alone Isn't Enough

One popular clothing retailer discovered that the more engaged its employees were, the worse the company performed! It was a case where the company had successfully created an in-store environment that supported its brand, and provided a specific experience for those who shopped and worked there. It was extremely congenial, workers were genuinely happy and helpful, the store looked fun and funky, and cool music boomed from hidden speakers. These were engaged employees doing what they did best, which was to create a positive, welcoming environment.

However, the retail chain's success in creating the right in-store vibe was offset by a lack of focus on their ultimate objective—which was to sell clothes. They didn't do enough in the area of sales training, they didn't focus on sales metrics, and they lacked a compensation system that supported sales performance. The company had done a great job hiring and rewarding nice and friendly people. But before long, it realized that what it needed to do was hire friendly people who also knew how to close sales on the latest fashions and discounts. This unusual retail situation shows that happy doesn't mean productive, and engagement alone isn't enough.

Rudy learned this lesson directly as he led Kenexa in the early 2000s. Kenexa managers were "eating their own dog food" as they say, and had created an environment that fostered trust and confidence, recognition and respect, growth and development; internal employee surveys showed that Kenexa workers were engaged. And yet, the company wasn't performing well financially. Things came to a head, during the recession of 2002, when Kenexa's biggest client went bankrupt and several Kenexa divisions were shrinking and losing money. Obviously, an engaged workforce was not enough to weather the storm.

In response to the crisis, Rudy stopped all compensation to the Kenexa leadership team and challenged them to regain their collective focus and discipline; their pay would resume once the hard decisions were made and the business was back on solid footing. It was during this time period that Kenexa seized upon a new mission—one that guides it still today—which is to help organizations identify the best individual for every job and to maximize their performance while in that job. Clarifying their core business enabled Kenexa leadership to execute the difficult but critical decisions to close or sell divisions that didn't fit and that were struggling financially. The team also implemented new tactics for measuring and communicating progress against monthly and quarterly objectives. With the new dual focus on both engagement and alignment to tightly defined objectives, Kenexa rebounded and completed its initial public offering (IPO) two years later, in 2005.

Alignment Is Critical

The earlier examples make the point that engaged employees without direction may give you retention benefits, but have little impact on business results. Organizational alignment simply means that people are voluntarily united to pursue a common cause. It suggests that all workers understand, agree, and work with the same understanding of the organization's core purpose, values, and objectives. Is your organization or team aligned? Try Activity 6.2. You might find the exercise enlightening, and maybe really amusing.

Activity 6.2   Alignment Speed Dial

STEP 1: The next time you are sitting at your desk at work, pick up the phone and call four people with whom you work closely on a daily basis. It could include your boss, a direct report, or several peers. Ask them these questions:
What do you think our core mission is?
How is what you are doing today supporting our mission?

STEP 2: Reflect on the answers you received. Did everyone pretty much describe the same mission (even if they put it into their own words)? Could they describe the link between their daily activities and the core purpose of the organization?

Did you really call your coworkers? If you asked people what your organization's mission or purpose is and they said something like, "Dude, what are you talking about?" you know you have a problem. If you asked how their work supports the organization's larger goals and they said, "Who knows and who cares?" you have a serious problem. Hopefully, even if they didn't get the official verbiage exactly right, they could describe both the big picture and how they are supporting it.

Some people have said to us that alignment is a euphemism for getting people to "drink the company Kool-Aid." That it implies a workforce of clones that lacks diversity and creativity, a place filled with yes-men and little innovation. This couldn't be farther from the truth. Alignment doesn't mean that everyone is marching the same way, in the same uniform, in lockstep. It means everyone knows which hill to climb, and *why* they are climbing that hill. How they make the climb is still up to them, and all talented performers are welcome to join the march. The benefits of alignment include:

- Elimination of waste—Organizational alignment eliminates the waste of time and resources associated with individuals and teams that are expending effort in areas that aren't mission critical.
- Performance improvement—Worker evaluation and accountability is easy once there are clear objectives; skills improve and training and development resources are invested in areas related to the core objectives.
- Increase in useable innovation—The collective creativity of all workers can be focused tightly, like a laser beam, on common objectives, thus increasing the amount of applied innovation.
- Talent improvement—Success begins early, in the recruiting and hiring process, as candidates are screened for alignment to values and objectives.

When it comes to the challenging job of executing on alignment, entire books have been written on the topic. What it comes down to is a handful of actions:

1. Be clear about your core purpose—Some call it an organization's mission, others define it as vision, and still others call it purpose. Senior leadership needs to define the purpose of the organization. Why are you all there? What are you trying to accomplish?
2. Cascade your objectives/goals—While your core purpose tells everyone what you're all about and provides general direction, alignment requires more concrete goals: at least annual and quarterly goals, if not monthly. A company's goals should

cascade down through the organization so every individual can quickly and easily know what their line of sight is to the big picture, and know whether they are succeeding or not.

3. Rhythm of communication—Just because you have your mission statement hanging in the lobby and individual objectives are tied to performance plans doesn't mean your team is aligned in that mission. With the fast pace and continuous changes that are now normal in our lives, you must aim to overcommunicate. Kevin and Rudy both have adopted the practice of short daily huddles with their management teams, along with monthly and quarterly meetings to share information and review progress against goals. Remember, communication should go in both directions; you should listen and learn as much as you inform. Using the communication rhythm described here means that information can go from a frontline worker to the CEO, and vice versa in 24 hours.

4. Reward success—Using the *We*-compensation approach of variable pay, all team members are given base pay but also variable pay that is tied to performance against goals. This is the motivator to stay focused and aligned. Additionally, the variable pay components should have elements tied to individual performance but also to team and organizational performance so you don't encourage purely selfish behaviors and too narrow a view of goals.

Harmonization

Harmony is beautiful to behold. It basically refers to separate things that occur simultaneously.

In music, harmony refers to when separate notes are played simultaneously. When three or more tones are played simultaneously, it's called a chord. Vocal harmonies consist of different singers singing different notes at the same time in the same song—different vocalists, uniquely contributing at the same time in the same song.

In American football, you can see harmony in the way 11 members of the offense execute a flawless play. A huddle is held so all members hear the play (i.e., the objective) and are clear on their contribution (their line of sight to the big picture). The nose guard snaps the ball to the quarterback, setting the play into motion. Eleven separate players execute their specific jobs. If even one of them fails, the likelihood of success plummets. The lone running back takes a fake handoff to freeze the defense for a second, a blindside block is made by the left tackle to prevent a sack, the quarterback throws the ball 20 yards down the field toward empty space, and a receiver suddenly breaks right and meets the ball that is already there. Separate players, simultaneous actions, all working toward a common goal. Harmony.

Harmonizing an organization works in the same way.

> Harmonization = Engagement + Alignment

Engagement is the catalyst to get you that extra edge in performance, while alignment ensures everyone is heading in the same direction.

Harmonization in a 1.2-Billion-Person Organization

Imagine you are the president of a fast-growing organization. In fact, you've been growing over 10 percent a year for three decades. Oh, and your organization has 1.2 billion people in it. Can you imagine how difficult your task is? How do you continue breakneck growth year after year? How do

(continued)

(continued)

you ensure that everyone in your fast-changing organization is engaged, productive, and cared for? How do you keep it all together? Of course, if you were presiding over such an organization, it wouldn't be a company. It would be China.

The world's fastest train shoots through central China at 250 miles per hour and is called the Harmony Express. This symbol of technological achievement and national pride was named after Chinese President Hu Jintao's signature vision called *harmonious society*. The slogan is ubiquitous throughout China, appearing on posters, billboards, in commercials on state-run TV and radio, and it has even crossed over to advertisements for the popular fast-food chain KFC. A harmonious society is viewed as the socioeconomic goal of the government (i.e., their BHAG) and changes China's focus from purely economic growth to overall societal balance.

The goal reflects the difficult tightrope walk of Chinese leadership. They must maintain the growth rate to provide jobs and prosperity, while at the same time addressing the gap between the urban wealthy and rural poor, environmental degradation, corruption, and the new demands of the 404 million primarily young Internet users.[3]

We don't need to be leading a global superpower to feel the pressure to balance competing interests. Great leaders are able to harmonize their organizations. Engaged, happy workers without discipline or focus on productivity goals are unsustainable. Achieving organizational goals and financial success with a disengaged workforce is unlikely. Harmonization at work consists of creating an environment that fosters engagement and harnesses the collective power of the workforce toward common goals.

One Person at a Time

While survey data of groups of workers reveal consistent truths, both engagement and alignment are activated throughout the world one person at a time, one interaction at a time. Every time you reach a team member, whether in a personal chat, e-mail, or large meeting, you have the opportunity to build trust, to share, to listen, and to align. Success in managing engagement and alignment requires, on the one hand, recognizing universal truths and then on the other hand, accepting unique differences. Organizations that are the most harmonized balance both successfully.

Chapter Summary

Harmonization = Engagement + Alignment
(You can download this summary as a one-page PDF at www.WeTheBook.com)

Employee engagement is the extent to which employees are motivated to contribute to organizational success and are willing to apply discretionary effort. It can be measured as a composite of four factors.

$$Engagement = Pride + Satisfaction +$$
$$Advocacy + Retention$$

But engagement alone isn't enough. You can have employees very engaged in their jobs, but if their efforts don't support their organization's mission and objectives, there will be no business benefit. People must also be aligned, which simply means that people are united in the pursuit of a common cause. Effective leaders successfully harmonize their teams.

$$Harmonization = Engagement + Alignment$$

(continued)

(*continued*)

Key Takeaways for Individuals

- Complete the four-question assessment of your current engagement level in this chapter. Are you fully engaged at work?
- Do you know how your daily activities contribute to the core mission of your organization? Do your quarterly objectives align with your company's objectives?

Key Takeaways for Managers

- Engagement is a catalyst but not the only answer. Alignment is vital but not enough. You must harmonize your team by driving both engagement and alignment.
- While the measures and drivers of engagement are globally universal, you must apply them with each individual, in every contact. There are no shortcuts.

Chapter Bonus Material

Rudy Karsan's Harmonization Speech in Shanghai

You have special access to material only available to readers of this book. Get Rudy Karsan's speech on Harmonization, which he delivered in Shanghai, China, in the summer of 2010.

1. Go to www.WeTheBook.com
2. Click the "Bonus Material" button/link
3. Click the link that says "Shanghai Speech"
4. Enter the password "harmony" (without the quotation marks)

Enjoy your bonus material!

Engagement Leads to "Better Earnings and Fatter Margins"

I believe there are many managers who have yet to grasp the essential connection between engagement and financial success. Companies that score highly on engagement have better earnings and fatter margins. . . .

—GARY HAMEL

Boost Earnings!

Earlier, we explored how employees' feelings at work impact all the other areas of their lives. But now we turn 180 degrees and show how employees' feelings about work impact the organizations they work for. And we don't just mean a warm and fuzzy impact; we mean cold, hard profit impact.

Imagine a gathering of corporate executives, huddled around a massive mahogany conference table, their company stock price falling, pressure from analysts and shareholders rising.

The impassioned CEO stands at the table and barks, "We need to increase profits 10 percent; now what are we going to do?!"

"Global expansion," proclaims one voice.

"Layoffs!" shouts another with gusto.

"Outsource IT," offers another.

"I'll renegotiate better rates," the CFO contributes.

And then one quiet but confident voice suggests, "Increase employee engagement." Heads turn, and you can hear a pin drop. . . .

Think about all the things companies do to increase profit or earnings per share. A simple Internet search on Google News for "boost earnings" pulls up these stories from a 24-hour period:

- Yahoo! enters a strategic partnership with Microsoft.
- Chevron to cut 2,000 jobs.
- Atmel to sell a chip factory.

151

- GE Healthcare expands business in India and China.
- Harrah's Entertainment pushes the payback date of $5.5 billion of loans.
- Applied Materials announces new stock buyback program.

But in the same 24-hour news cycle, there isn't one story about a major corporation improving employee engagement.

The point of the opening, obviously contrived, story isn't that actions like cutting costs, selling underperforming assets, or striking partnerships are wrong; executives should use all the tools at their disposal to maximize returns. And *that* is actually the point. They should use *all* the tools they have available. Employee engagement often isn't considered a boardroom-level topic, because many leaders don't realize that it is as critical to the bottom line as many other tactics.

"What do you mean, increase employee engagement?" the CEO asks, with one eyebrow raised.

The young executive across the table knows this is her opening. She makes the most of it: "I have solid research that shows the difference between an engaged workforce and a disengaged one can mean a 22-point difference in total shareholder returns."

The CEO sits down and breathes deeply. He smiles cautiously, "Go ahead, tell me more."

Mirror, Mirror, On the Wall . . .

Southwest Airlines founder and former CEO, Herb Kelleher, used to repeat his secret to success like a mantra, "You have to treat your employees like your customers." Kelleher's simple statement said in nine words what dozens of business researchers have described in hundreds of pages published in the *Harvard Business Review* and elsewhere.

In the classic 1997 business book, *The Service Profit Chain*, James Heskett and W. Earl Sasser coined the term *employee customer satisfaction mirror*. It's the positive correlation many researchers have found between *customer* satisfaction and *employee* satisfaction. It's called a mirror because it's believed that the process works both ways. You might observe the existence of the mirror yourself in everyday transactions. Complete Activity 7.1 to explore how the mirror works.

Activity 7.1 Who Is Making Whom Happy?

INSTRUCTIONS: Imagine an interaction in a restaurant between the waiter and his customer. First, imagine you are the customer, and read the story on the left. Then, imagine you're the waiter and read the story on the right.

Question: Did the waiter's cheerful demeanor make the customer feel good? Or did the customer's friendliness, manners, and tip cheer up the waiter?

Delighted customers make employees feel good about their company and work, and engaged workers make customers more satisfied.

Beyond Customer Service

But Heskett and Sasser didn't call their book *The Satisfaction Mirror*; they called it *The Service Profit Chain*. This is because the satisfaction mirror is just one part—perhaps the key part—of the bigger chain that ultimately causes engagement to lead to profits. Put simply, the linkage in the chain goes like this: Engaged and productive employees drive better service. Good service drives customer satisfaction. Customer satisfaction drives customer loyalty, which in turn drive profits and growth. Figure 7.1 depicts a simplified model of this chain.

Let's look at employee engagement first. It goes without saying that no company, small or large, can win over the long run without energized employees who believe in the mission and understand how to achieve it.[1]

—Jack and Suzy Welch

And, of course, there is one final link in the chain that goes beyond profit. Over the long term the two biggest factors in the value of a company, represented in public companies by its stock price, are profitability and the company's growth rate. So you can add *total*

Figure 7.1 The Service Profit Chain

Figure 7.2 The Engagement Shareholder Value Chain

shareholder value as an additional outcome of employee engagement, reflected in our simplified model, as shown in Figure 7.2.

The True Cost of Turnover

The financial impact of employee turnover cannot be overstated. When someone voluntarily leaves your company, the direct costs include separation tasks, possible legal fees, recruiting, onboarding, and training. But among the executive ranks and in companies that are comprised primarily of service workers, the real cost of turnover is the indirect productivity hit you take while the new replacement is getting up to speed. The hidden costs associated with the new hire learning curve include errors made on the job, substantial disruption of supervisors and peers, slower service response times, and a lower closing ratio on sales.

Even among the most basic entry-level positions, the cost of turnover can be substantial. One rigorous study conducted by researchers at Cornell looked at turnover across four different hotels, examining direct and indirect costs for replacing various positions, including front desk associates, cooks, gift shop clerks, and room service wait staff. They found that the true cost of turnover ranged from 29 to 38 percent of annual pay.[2]

Focusing on other occupations, studies have indicated that the true cost of turnover for registered nurses is over $64,000,[3] and that it costs almost $22,000 to replace a $13 per hour call center agent.[4]

Of course, a disengaged employee doesn't always leave your company. When it comes to employee retention, there is a push-friction-pull dynamic. The push element of the dynamic refers to the disengagement that makes the employee more inclined to look for a new job or more susceptible to outside recruiters; you are pushing them out the door. The pull element refers to external opportunities provided by another employer; they are pulling them away from you. Employees may leave because of an opportunity for better compensation, faster advancement, better work-life balance, or a combination of various factors. But just because there is a push, a pull, or even both, that doesn't mean they will actually resign. The friction refers to the things that interfere with a person's desire to leave. Those inhibitors might include uncertainty, the value of existing at work relationships, family situations, and the possibility that a spouse may need employment if the new job requires relocation.

Driving High Performance Culture at A.P. Moller-Maersk

Every organization can benefit from gathering candid feedback from its employees. However, when you have more than 110,000 people, working in 20 different businesses areas, speaking 100 different languages, and spread across 130 countries, the task of gathering that feedback becomes considerably more complex. That is the challenge Danish conglomerate, A.P. Moller-Maersk, takes on each year.

"We want to be the first choice employer for top performers," said Thomas Hedegaard Rasmussen, General Manager of Group Human Resources. "We created the engagement survey as a mechanism for employees to voice their opinions about their work, about the organization and about their managers. By understanding what engages our best performers, we're able to create a stimulating workplace and to attract and retain the best talent."

The engagement survey, crafted by Kenexa and translated into 16 languages, is administered in September each year. The majority of employees complete the survey online, after their direct manager e-mails them a Web link. Paper surveys are provided to those who do not have access to a computer. These are then shipped back to Kenexa for analysis. All responses are anonymous and remain confidential.

In 2006, the first engagement survey achieved an 80 percent response rate. This has steadily improved and in 2009, the response rate was 89 percent. "People like to participate in the survey and give their input," said Rasmussen. "We learn what is important to them, where we're doing well, and what we can do better. It's like holding up a mirror to the organization and the findings form the basis of a wide range of decisions."

As a direct result of the survey, A.P. Moller-Maersk has introduced local and group-wide improvements in its 20 businesses, in areas such as retention, leadership, teamwork, performance, communication, innovation, and organizational change. "We use the engagement survey to improve the workplace, to focus our attention on key interventions, and to track progress," said Rasmussen. "Because it is undertaken in consecutive years, we're able to review the impact of these interventions, monitor trends, and compare results with how we scored in previous years."

The survey shows that A.P. Moller-Maersk has highly engaged employees who are proud to work for the group, and that engagement is clearly linked to retention. However, it does more than measure the temperature of the organization. Employees are also asked to assess their direct manager. Over the past year, an index of 13 items measuring employee perceptions of their manager's effectiveness has risen from 69 percent favorable to

73 percent. "To win in the marketplace, we need great leaders," said Rasmussen. "The feedback from the engagement survey is one of the tools we use to help our leaders to develop and improve. It's an opportunity to assess how they are performing and to gain feedback on the effectiveness of our leadership courses."

"The engagement survey results are worthless if we don't share them," said Rasmussen. "We communicate the results throughout the business." At the group leadership level, comparisons between the 20 different business units are reviewed and the performance and engagement scores are benchmarked against Kenexa's database of the top 25 percent of high performing companies in the Global 500, *Fortune* magazine's list of the world's biggest companies. Group-wide focus areas for the coming year are then developed. At the business unit level, best practice is shared and the survey results are used to launch and monitor key initiatives. At the team level, individual employees meet with their leader to go through the engagement results and to develop an action plan for improvement over the coming year.

A.P. Moller-Maersk will continue to utilize the engagement survey in its quest to become the preferred supplier in its markets. "Engagement is at the heart of many things that we do," said Rasmussen. "The survey gives our employees the chance to air their views and we've been able to drive high performance by taking onboard their feedback. In an economic downturn, your business results depend on having engaged employees who perform well and good leaders who ask the right questions."

Kennametal Conducts a Survey in Turbulent Economic Times

Headquartered in Latrobe, Pennsylvania, Kennametal Inc. (NYSE: KMT) is a leading global supplier of tooling, engineered components, and advanced materials consumed in production processes. Companies producing everything from airframes to coal, from medical implants to oil wells, and from turbochargers to motorcycle parts recognize Kennametal for extraordinary contributions to its value chains. As of the prior fiscal year-end, customers bought approximately $2.7 billion annually of Kennametal products and services—delivered by 13,000 talented employees in more than 60 countries—with 50 percent of these revenues coming from outside North America.

Like the general economy, Kennametal is experiencing some financial shortfalls. Business is down across markets, regions, and every sector it operates, resulting in layoffs throughout the enterprise and other cost-cutting measures such as work furloughs where employees are asked to take time off without pay. Even through these challenging times, one area that is retaining sharp focus is a commitment to taking actions to maintain employee engagement and motivation.

"In 2006, Kennametal wanted to make significant strides in becoming an employer of choice for the best people," explained Kevin Walling, vice president and chief human resources officer at Kennametal. "One of the best practices we discovered was to conduct employee engagement surveys to get into the hearts and minds of our people."

Kennametal selected Kenexa to help with the survey design and implementation based on the company's track record, global experience, and the relationship that developed through the review process. Kenexa's Employee Engagement Surveys measure attitudes that drive behavior, which in turn drive business results. The survey process culminates in hard data on the barriers and opportunities to employees becoming more engaged.

"The executive and management teams at Kennametal realized that it was imperative that we hear from our employees both in good times and bad," continued Walling. "In 2006, we made a global commitment to our workforce that their feedback was critical. We also realized that feedback was going to help us ultimately not only create a great place to work, but deliver for our shareholders, customers, and partners."

Reactions from the workforce to conducting a survey during these turbulent times were both positive and negative. In both North America and Europe, external and internal workgroups questioned Kennametal's decision to conduct the survey amid the current economic conditions. The company's CEO, Carlos Cardoso, personally responded and spoke of the importance of reaching out to every employee, understanding his or her perspective, and making the work environment better, safer, and more productive. In turn, these groups supported the survey.

"Making the decision to continue with the survey was a powerful nonverbal message to our employees that we cared," said Walling. "Even in tough times, our employees understood that this organization is committed to improving and moving forward with making our organization a desired employer of choice."

From the first survey, Kennametal learned it had to focus on improved communication and to develop a taskforce to determine how to make improvements on multiple fronts. It created specific executive actions and communication programs, leadership toolkits, and an executive blog hosted by the CEO on the corporate intranet, as well as some plant-specific employee feedback tools.

"The result of this was that we recognized a 16 percent improvement in our communication score, which was very significant," said Walling. "Our overall engagement score remained the same from the first survey. What that says is that despite the challenging business environment and economic challenges we are facing, the discipline to improve a key driver of engagement (organizational communication) enables us to endure these challenges and ensure the long-term success of our employees and the enterprise."

Walling notes that with this most recent survey, the key driver has changed and Kennametal is now focused on providing more about the future vision of the company. Adds Christina Reitano, corporate communications manager at Kennametal, "We are using a lot of the communication programs we created out of the first survey to communicate with our employees during these difficult times. Our CEO's blog gets around 7,000 unique visitors each month. Considering that most of our workforce is manufacturing-based and not sitting at a computer, that response is amazing."

With the results of its second survey in hand, the next step is working with Kennametal's top executives to create alignment at the executive level to what employees are saying. In addition to providing support and advice on what actions to endorse at the executive level, Kenexa also provided support to train and develop capability for other people throughout the organization to analyze their results.

"Having the survey as a platform, we now have the foundation on which to quickly and accurately get a read on our employees," said Walling. "This is a competitive advantage, particularly in challenging times because we're not guessing. As survey results provide us with greater insight about the key drivers of our employee engagement, we will be able to get quicker and better outcomes with our organizational initiatives.

Aetna Demands Proof; Results from a 39-Company Study

Aetna has been one of the best-known names in the insurance industry for more than 150 years, but in 2000 the company experienced significant business failure. Under new leadership in 2001, Aetna engineered one of the most successful corporate turnarounds in recent U.S. history. Over a five-year period, Aetna's shareholders were rewarded with a stock price increase of more than 600 percent.

By the end of 2007, Aetna was vying for industry leadership, and with help from Kenexa it developed a new employee engagement index to help take the company to the next level. Like the fictional CEO at the beginning of this chapter, Aetna CEO Ron Williams was interested in understanding whether the employee engagement index was just a cultural marker, or one that actually correlated to financial results.

Since achieving consistent operating performance to improve shareholder value and restoring investor confidence have been important themes for Aetna, total shareholder return (TSR) was a logical measure of performance. TSR is a concept used to compare the performance of different companies over time by combining share price appreciation and dividends paid.

Next, an analysis was needed of a comparable group of publicly held companies that asked matching employee survey questions, and for which TSR measures could be derived. Aetna turned to Kenexa to help conduct the analysis and find an answer. Thirty-nine organizations were identified for inclusion in the study based on those parameters. Relationships among one-year and five-year TSR were examined with respect to employee engagement (as an index) and the four independent items that comprise the index. The average scores of these items, the engagement index, and the one-year and five-year TSR values had a fair amount of variability across all 39 organizations.

Employing traditional linkage analyses the correlation between TSR and the employee engagement index was found to be 0.45, a moderate to strong level of correlation. To better understand what was happening at the varying levels of employee engagement across the sample, the sample was divided into some commonly used normative percentile markers, namely the bottom 25 percent, 50th percentile, and top 25 percent. It was found that organizations that scored in the top 25 percent on employee engagement had a five-year TSR of 17.93 percent, and companies in the bottom 25 percent had an average TSR of negative 4.13 percent. Put another way, the five-year TSR gap between the most and least engaged workforces was a whopping 22 points (see Figure 7.3).

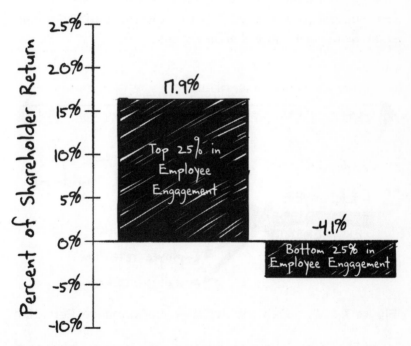

Figure 7.3 Five-Year Total Shareholder Return Between Top and Bottom Performing Companies in Employee Engagement

Engagement Isn't the *Only* Answer

Researchers have shown repeatedly that employee engagement isn't just a human resources or personnel initiative, but a strategic imperative that drives real business outcomes. There is an indisputable linkage between employee engagement and productivity, retention, client service—all of which drive increases in profitability and shareholder value. And, of course, the converse is true. Employee *disengagement* in the United States alone costs hundreds of billions of dollars each year in lost productivity.

However, as mentioned earlier, if an employee is in the wrong job or is happy completing misaligned tasks, engagement will not contribute to the company's success. To maximize success, engaged workers need to act in alignment and contribute en masse to organizational achievement.

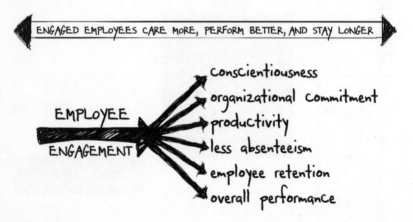

Figure 7.4   Engagement on Caring, Performance, Retention

Chapter Summary

Better Earnings and Fatter Margins

(You can download this summary as a one-page PDF at www .WeTheBook.com)

Employee engagement has a material impact on retention, service, and productivity. These factors, in turn, drive customer satisfaction and loyalty, which are the key drivers to growth and profit, finally impacting shareholder value.

"There is a five times greater difference in shareholder value between the companies with the most engaged workers and the least."[5]

Key Takeaways for Individuals

- Your engagement level doesn't just impact you; it impacts the quality of your work and interactions with customers.
- If you work in an organization with a toxic culture and disengaged employees, it will be difficult for the organization to achieve financial success over the long term.

Key Takeaways for Managers

- Employee engagement is not the same thing as employee satisfaction.
- Employee engagement isn't just a soft measure of culture; it's a critical link in the service to profit chain.
- When was the last time you measured your team's engagement index? More importantly, when was the last time you acted on the results?

Chapter Bonus Material

Audio Interviews with Business Leaders on Engagement

You have special access to material only available to readers of this book. Listen to business leaders explain how employee engagement drives real business results in their organizations.

1. Go to www.WeTheBook.com
2. Click the "Bonus Material" button/link
3. Click the link that says "Leaders Discuss Engagement"
4. Enter the password "profit" (without the quotation marks)

Enjoy your bonus material!

Part Four

Manager's Toolkit

By now you're convinced of the power of a fully engaged work-force. You get it: Higher employee engagement can lead to higher levels of service, quality, and productivity, which in turn lead to higher growth, profit, and shareholder return.

But how do you actually do it?

How can you, as a manager, engage your workers?

How can you take a disengaged workforce, and turn them around?

This section provides the answers to those questions. It offers tools that you can use *today*, in the form of questions to ask team members and action items you can deploy to begin making progress. Remember, while the drivers of engagement are largely universal, the areas of your focus will be driven by your unique circumstances. And while people are people, engagement is built—even earned—one person at a time.

8

GReAT Managers Focus on Growth, Recognition, And Trust

There is more hunger for love and appreciation in this world than there is for bread.

—MOTHER TERESA

There is no single driver of engagement that applies universally. People care about different things. Some might be driven by verbal recognition while others might be inspired by a bold vision, and still others may be driven by enjoyment of the great team they work with. But while there is no single silver bullet, Kenexa's global surveys of over 10 million workers each year, and our own experience as leaders, tell us that three drivers consistently rank at the top of the list for most people. These are growth, recognition, and trust, and you can remember these factors with the word GReAT. As in, "GReAT managers focus on Growth, Recognition, And Trust." This chapter explores just how these drivers cause people to be engaged at work.

Growth

Growth itself contains the germ of happiness.

—Pearl Buck

When we talk about growth and development, we're referring to how satisfied employees are with progress toward their career objectives and about their access to learning and developmental opportunities within the organization. This is an important concept to think about, because when employees are satisfied with their development, they are more likely to have higher loyalty, motivation, commitment, and overall satisfaction, all of which adds to improved performance. Kenexa research shows the strong link between perceptions of growth and retention. In fact, half of all workers who feel that their skills are stagnating indicate that they plan to leave their employer within one to two years.

Many think growth and development simply means more training. In fact, this belief is at the root of many worker-employer conflicts on this issue. Senior management might focus on all the time and money spent on formal training programs, which is good, but employees may be looking for more informal opportunities for growth. These can include having a mentor at the company, time on the job to pursue new interests, assignments, or tasks that are challenging, higher visibility opportunities, access to internal job openings, and a formal career path process.

It's an unfortunate reality that many managers believe there is a risk associated with training employees beyond the skills needed for the immediate job. They believe the new skills will make the employee more marketable, which will increase the likelihood that he or she will leave the company. "Why should I spend money in my budget to train them for a job with my competition?" they might think.

Quite simply, the data doesn't support this fear. In response to the survey question, "If I left my current job, my skills would allow me to find a similar job," 11 percent of those who responded unfavorably indicate that they will be leaving within a year; this number changes to only 13 percent for those who respond favorably.[1] In other words, there is virtually no difference on someone's intent to leave for another job between those who feel that their skills are current and those who feel that their skills are dated. Providing training and opportunities for further development does not make it more likely that they will use their new skills to leave for another company.

In addition to specific tactics to drive growth and development, you may want to focus on managing the employee-role within the reality of the organization's structure and growth. It's always a good idea to let employees know where they stand and set realistic expectations for meeting their career objectives. This is especially true for your high-performing, promotion-ready employees when there are currently limited promotion opportunities. It is also important to develop a plan for keeping employees who are not interested in any position changes interested in the company.

Survey Items that Measure Growth and Development

The types of statements that are included in surveys to measure growth and development include:

1. I can achieve my career goals at this company.
2. This company provides me with the opportunities for growth and development.
3. I am given a real opportunity to improve my skills in my company.

If you suspect that your direct reports are not satisfied with their career growth or development, use the following Kenexa Focused Listening Questions to guide your dialogue with them.

1. In general, do you think that most people are satisfied with their opportunities for career growth and development within our organization? If no, why not?

2. What additional career growth or development opportunities would you like to see in order to maximize your potential?
3. When was the last time you were provided the opportunity to receive additional, job-related training?

Let the answers to the Kenexa Focused Listening Questions guide your actions as a leader. Some generic ideas for how you can increase your team members' perceptions about your interest in their career growth and development include:

1. Make professional development the topic of one of your meetings with your direct reports, and discuss the following issues:
   - What knowledge, skills, and abilities are most critical to their job.
   - What needs to be developed and how you, as the manager, can support those needs.
   - What development gaps there are between current and desired skills.
   - What suggestions, ideas, and coaching on how to fill those gaps you can provide.
2. Schedule career conferences with each employee. Discuss short and long-term goals, potential obstacles to success, and the resources needed. Assist the employee to visualize his or her career three and five years from now and identify the skills and opportunities needed to advance. Ask your employees to set up quarterly progress meetings with you to keep updated on their goals and how you can support them in their development.
3. Conduct a training audit of your team. After clarifying the specific goals of each individual, discuss and assess their training needs. Establish a complete list of individuals' goals and

prioritize the list based on the needs of the organization and the talents of the people. Identify costs and utilize appropriate channels to determine which training needs can be met. Communicate the final decisions and rationale. Discuss next steps and possible timetables for additional training opportunities in the future.

Additionally, you may want to focus on managing the employee-role within the reality of your organization's structure and growth. Growth becomes relatively easy when the organization itself is expanding rapidly and opening up new job positions. It can be a real challenge in a small organization that isn't growing, or even worse, in an organization that is experiencing downsizing. Let employees know where they stand and set realistic expectations for meeting their career objectives. Again, this is especially true for your high-performing, promotion-ready employees when there are currently limited promotion opportunities.

Recognition

A soldier will fight long and hard for a bit of colored ribbon.

—NAPOLEON BONAPARTE

Showing recognition and appreciation costs nothing and has a dramatic impact on employee engagement. Yet, in one Kenexa survey of 20,000 employees in 14 countries, only 47 percent of respondents said they were satisfied with the recognition they received from their managers.[2] This shows that this particular driver still has vast potential to be used effectively in organizations around the world.

Valuing versus Recognizing Employees

Jeffrey Jolton, Ph.D., Kenexa

There is currently a lot of interest in recognition programs. A Google search on "employee recognition" churns out more than 900,000 hits. Recognition is one of those principles of people management about which we are routinely reminded, and frankly, should be reminded about, because it can always be done better and more often.

The best organizations spend a substantial amount of money and resources on their recognition program. One only needs to look at the number of Google hits on "recognition" to see how many are related to employee awards and services being sold. Despite these investments, employees don't necessarily feel they are being recognized for great work.

One of the more common statements found on employee engagement surveys is some variation of, "I receive recognition when I do good work." The norm across industries and countries for this question is about 55 percent favorable. Meaning, on average, about half of all employees feel they are appropriately recognized. At the best companies—the top 10 percent—the score is about 66 percent favorable, not overly impressive when these companies have favorable scores in the 80 to 90 percent range in a number of other areas.

Compare this to the inquiry, "I feel valued as an employee of this company," which is much less frequently asked (indicating that many organizations don't even see the value in asking about employees feeling valued). On average, less than half of the employees in a typical organization feel valued and one-third actively believe they aren't valued at all. The average score here is 41 percent favorable, with 32 percent of participants responding unfavorably. These findings also indicate that there is a difference between recognizing and valuing employees. As a whole, organizations are especially weak in creating an environment where employees truly feel valued.

This is more than a difference in semantics; it's a difference in experience. Recognition is the identification or acknowledgment of an achievement. When we recognize employees, we acknowledge that they are doing good work and let them know we appreciate their efforts. Recognition is typically tied to what we do—not who we are.

Valuing is about appreciating the worth of something (someone) and of esteeming something (someone) highly. When we value employees, we appreciate them for who they are and what they bring to the organization. We acknowledge them not merely for tasks, but for the deeper intrinsic worth they add to the organization by just being there. Recognizing an individual is done when they've successfully completed a project. Valuing someone is letting him or her know that you are glad that person is on the team.

Research from several Kenexa clients, which have included both value and recognition items in their surveys, shows that, in general, valuing employees appears to be a driver of engagement (and often the top driver), more often than recognizing their efforts. In a limited sample of companies, feeling valued showed up as a driver 85 percent of the time, whereas recognition of efforts emerged only 30 percent of the time. Feeling valued seems to reflect a broad

(*continued*)

(*continued*)

core of what people are looking for in an engaging work experience—that is, a primary element that connects people to their organization and motivates them at work is a strong sense of feeling valued and appreciated. Recognition is important, but it is more likely to be seen as a singular experience (event driven) than sustained (environment driven).

The two behaviors are interactive, however. Organizations that had high scores on valuing employees had higher scores on recognizing employees. But recognizing efforts didn't always translate to people feeling valued.

Looking at dysfunctional organizations, one characteristic that emerges for some is rote recognition. These companies recognize people for anything and everything with no real purpose or thought behind it. It is as if someone was told, "recognition equals engagement" and so he or she just ran around patting everyone on the back saying "good job" regardless of the real effort or accomplishment achieved. This underscores the importance of showing your people you value, not just recognize, them.

Recognition without value, over time, will make the recognition hollow. It turns something that should be satisfying and special to employees into something rote and meaningless. Furthermore, without valuing employees, organizations fall into a dangerous zone where they fail to treat and see employees as people.

Valuing others isn't a leadership thing; it's a people thing, and it is probably the people thing that the majority of us cherish the most. If you think back to a moment in your life when you felt special and appreciated, it's most likely a time when you were being valued in some way.

Looking across eight companies of different sizes and industries, the following common behaviors emerged that promote higher ratings of value and recognition:

- Recognize real contributions—when someone does something exceptional, let them know.
- Show respect—treat people as you want to be treated; don't yell, belittle, trivialize, patronize, or deceive.
- Empower decision making—give people input into the decisions that affect their work the most; make them a part of the decision-making process.
- Explain why they are important—discuss how one's role and contributions fit into the overall success of the company.
- Explain rather than tell—avoid dictating change and process to employees; let them understand the reasons behind things.
- Look at team performance—don't focus solely on individual contributions, but also note how team efforts contributed to overall success.
- Train supervisors—day-to-day recognition can be expressed effectively by immediate supervisors, but make sure they know how to give recognition appropriately.
- Ensure job performance and pay are linked—people should feel that the effort they put forth is reflected in their pay.

(*continued*)

(*continued*)

- Be transparent and fair—let people know why others are receiving recognition or promotion opportunities and avoid favoritism.
- Build a culture of celebration over competition—encourage everyone to celebrate an individual's or team's success.

We can all do a better job of valuing those around us. For those doing the valuing, it's not only rewarding; it's where you feel the most vulnerable. This is why we don't do it as often as we should. Instead, we censor ourselves—fearing our comments might be used against us. In most cases, it's not a warranted fear, and the gains far outweigh any potential risk in making one's deep appreciation of others known.

Recognition tends to be a public action, while appreciation is often a private one. Military organizations throughout history have shown the power of recognition to motivate. The Romans recognized the contributions of the soldiers with rewards for their bravery; the highest individual award was the "civic crown," made of oak leaves, given for saving the life of a fellow soldier on the battlefield. After the American Revolutionary War, General Washington gave a chevron on the left sleeve of all veterans who had served three years with bravery, fidelity, and good conduct. In 1900, Queen Victoria authorized the wearing of the shamrock on St. Patrick's Day, due to the tremendous public sentiment produced by the gallantry of the Irish troops in the Boer War.

Yet, the concept of recognition versus appreciation can be highlighted in the unfortunate times when a soldier dies in combat. While a medal awarded posthumously is recognition well deserved, in the long term, the family will probably value more a personal letter from the commanding officer or a visit from a fellow soldier who shares how his ultimate sacrifice helped the other men in his unit.

Or, to consider an example from the business world, imagine a programmer who works evenings and weekends to complete a project on deadline. She may enjoy the recognition that comes from being named Employee of the Month, but she will feel more appreciated from personal words of gratitude from her manager, or if the manager writes a letter to the senior executives explaining the value of her extra effort.

The feeling of appreciation is internal to the employee and can be generated in a variety of ways. Rudy has a friend who took a job as an immigration officer at Pearson International Airport in Toronto, shortly after graduating from college. The work environment was rigid and hierarchical and offered very little in the form of recognition and nothing remotely in the form of appreciation. As a junior officer, it was very difficult to understand what constituted a job well done. Was it speed in processing the visitors? Certainly, on the rare occasion that an officer uncovered false documents or apprehended a person on the watch list, a pat on the back was earned. Recognition was rare but possible; appreciation was a foreign concept.

One day this young officer met and processed a young immigrant woman and her daughter from Poland. It was a case he had worked on before they arrived and had expedited as best he could, given the fact that the woman and child had been separated from their husband and father, who had arrived in Canada one year earlier. After closing the file and sending them on their way, the immigration officer took his afternoon break and decided to go to a coffee shop near the international arrivals section of the airport. As he was walking, he saw the woman he had just processed beaming with joy, with tears streaming down her face. He followed her gaze to a man moving toward her about 20 feet away. He, too, was crying as he fought his way through the crowd to sweep his wife and child into his arms.

No one thanked this officer for his small part in reuniting this family. It was enough for him to witness their joy. No words were spoken, but what he observed made him feel immensely valued. In fact, this chance encounter changed his outlook on his career in the immigration department. Within a few months, he earned a promotion to a position that allowed him to interact with immigrants and refugees at a more personal and meaningful level. Instead of leaving before his one-year anniversary as planned, he spent a much longer period of time there before moving on. This drama repeats itself many times per day in airports throughout North America. It would be a simple thing for a supervisor to lead a new officer into the arrivals section to observe the outcome of their work, but it's unlikely that they will ever do this.

Survey Items that Measure Recognition and Respect

The types of survey statements that are used to measure recognition and respect include:

1. Where I work, employees are recognized for delivering outstanding customer service.
2. This company values my contribution.
3. This company recognizes productive people.

If you suspect that your direct reports are not satisfied with the type or extent of recognition they receive, or if you hear them criticize your organization's current recognition program as not being meaningful or the rewards as being insufficient, use the following Kenexa Focused Listening Questions to guide your dialogue with them to find out what's wrong.

1. Does management give recognition to employees who deliver outstanding customer service? How?
2. When do you feel valued as an employee? What do you feel valued for?
3. What are some ways your manager and our organization can do a better job at recognizing and rewarding outstanding performance?

Let the answers to the Kenexa Focused Listening Questions guide your actions as a leader. Some generic ideas for how you can increase your team members' feelings of being respected and recognized include:

1. Using the Focused Listening Questions as a basis, initiate a discussion with your employees about how successes should be recognized and rewarded. Discover the type of recognition that would be most meaningful to different employees and keep a record of this information for future reference.
2. Give public recognition to employees for jobs well done. When possible, tie employees' accomplishments to the bigger picture so that employees understand how their efforts impact the team and the company as a whole.
3. Make a practice of praising and promoting your employees to your superiors. When possible, do so in front of the employee. When praising and promoting an employee to a superior via e-mail, "Cc" the employee or provide them with a hardcopy of the e-mail.

Do not forget that while nonmonetary recognition is powerful, it cannot replace periodic and competitive pay raises and occasional monetary rewards, which are both critical pieces in an effective recognition program. You can't consider recognition programs to be a way to save money on compensation.

Trust

Trust is the essence of leadership.

—COLIN POWELL

When there is a strong degree of trust and confidence in senior leaders, employee engagement increases. Our research has found that across the globe, trust affects many other workplace behaviors and outcomes, including communication, helping behaviors, negotiation processes, conflict resolution, satisfaction, commitment, and acceptance of goals.

We all know from personal experience that trust is essential for any relationship to be successful. No relationship, personal or business, can flourish for even a short period of time if some element of trust is not present. But what exactly is trust and how can leaders build and sustain higher levels of trust from their employees?

The Three Cs of Building Trust

Peter Timmerman, Ph.D., Kenexa

Trust can be defined as the willingness to be vulnerable to the actions of a leader based on the expectation that the leader will take action in a manner that is important to the employee. Note that trust is not a behavior (e.g., cooperation), a choice (e.g., taking a risk), or a feeling (e.g., confidence). Rather, trust is a state of mind (i.e., a willingness to be vulnerable) that can result in being cooperative, taking risks, and feeling confident. The foundation of trust is built primarily on the characteristics of the person being trusted (i.e., a leader).

Research has identified three characteristics of a leader that will lead the person to be more or less trusted. These characteristics are the foundation for the development of trust. Perceptions of the leader's

1. Competence
2. Care
3. Commitment

are known as the "three Cs of trust"; these are the building blocks to pursue.

Competence has been defined as a "group of skills, abilities, and characteristics that enable a party to have influence within some specific domain." Thus, competence is domain-specific such that the leader may be highly competent is some areas, but have little aptitude, training, or experience in another area. For example, a leader may be trusted because of his or her ability to manage complex situations, but not trusted to interact effectively with an important customer. I once worked with a manager who had a dismal manager effectiveness score on a recent survey. When I met with her employees to discuss their managers' scores, they complained that their manager was incompetent in working with several computer programs that they themselves were required to use on a daily basis. Whenever a new employee

(continued)

(*continued*)

joined the group, the manager always assigned a veteran employee to train the new employee on the computer programs. While the manager may have thought of this as appropriate delegation of responsibility, it undermined her employees' trust in her because they perceived her as being incompetent in one of her core responsibilities.

Care is the extent to which a leader is believed to want to do good to the employee, aside from an egocentric profit motive. A leader's goodwill and display of genuine concern for an employee fosters an attachment to the leader and the perception of the leader as being trustworthy. A classic example of care would be the helpfulness and assistance that a mentor would provide to a protégé, in which the mentor is motivated only by concern for the protégé. One of the best managers I had went to bat for me to the organization's leadership for a pay raise. While there was an agreement with the senior leadership that I would receive the raise when I reached a certain milestone, my manager argued that my workload had impeded my ability to meet the milestone and he negotiated an agreement that I would receive half of the raise immediately and the other half when the milestone was achieved. The partial raise went into effect shortly after, even though my manager stood to gain nothing from my benefit.

Perceptions of commitment evolve when the leader is believed to consistently follow a set of values or principles to which employees agree. Research has found that perceptions of leaders' commitment are developed when that person acts consistently, displays a strong sense of justice, and when his actions are congruent with his words. A friend of mine worked for a manager who once gave him a specific direction and then, behind my friend's back, threw him under the bus to other organizational managers for fulfilling the direction. My friend confronted his manager who, in turn, denied his behavior. My friend was never able to trust his manager again, and to this day, thinks very little of the manager.

As a manager and a leader, you have tremendous opportunities to enable your employees to remain engaged even during some of the most difficult and trying times. However, your efforts will be undermined if employees perceive you as untrustworthy. In your daily interactions with employees, remember the three Cs: capitalize on the opportunities to demonstrate your competency in the core responsibilities, care for employees, and keep your commitments in word and in deed.

Trust and confidence in one's leaders are important drivers of employee engagement. This encompasses both the trust and confidence the leader or manager evokes in the employee and the trust and confidence the employee has in the future success of the organization.

If you suspect that your direct reports do not have confidence in you or the organization's leadership or future, use the following Kenexa Focused Listening Questions to guide your dialogue with them.

1. How can our leadership team foster greater trust among the employees?
2. How strong is the employees' level of confidence in our senior leadership?
3. If you were invited to consult our senior leadership on how to improve their job performance, what would you tell them?

Survey Items that Measure Trust and Confidence

The types of survey statements that are used to measure trust and confidence include:

1. I trust the leadership of this company.
2. I have confidence in my company's senior leaders.
3. Leadership at this company has the ability to deal with the challenges we face.

Let the answers to the Kenexa Focused Listening Questions guide your actions as a leader. Some generic ideas for how you can increase your team members' feelings of trust and confidence include:

1. Three key antecedents of being perceived as trustworthy are ability, benevolence, and integrity. Evaluate how trustworthy your employees may perceive you by asking yourself the following questions: (1) Am I competent in managing my department and in making sound decisions? (2) Do I set clear expectations and directions? (3) Do I show by word and deed that I'm honest and can be trusted? (4) Do my decisions and actions show genuine concern and respect for my employees?

2. Integrity tips: When you make a mistake, acknowledge it, correct it, and take steps to prevent its reoccurrence. When someone takes you into his or her confidence, maintain it; if you cannot maintain the confidence, say so up front. Make sure others get the credit they deserve, and when in doubt, share the credit anyway. If you are a manager, remember that you are accountable for both your own performance and the

performance of your group. When the group fails to live up to the company's mission, vision, and values, avoid placing blame on others. People watch what you do more than what you say; failing to fulfill a commitment will be remembered longer than the excuses offered.

3. Request that your employees anonymously submit a list of your most effective qualities as a leader, and equally important, a list of your qualities that undermine your effectiveness as a leader. Pick one or two of the ineffective qualities and develop a plan to minimize their influence. Inform your team members of your plan and ask for feedback on your progress.

It takes a lot of self-awareness to judge your own competence, empathy for your teammates, and track record of keeping commitments. As a manager, you should be mindful of your own performance in these areas and seek candid feedback from others on how you can improve your leadership abilities.

Chapter Summary

On Growth, Recognition, and Trust

(You can download this summary as a one-page PDF at www .WeTheBook.com)

The "big three" drivers of employee engagement are Growth, Recognition, and Trust, which appear consistently as the top factors in the world. The knowledge that they can have confidence and trust in their leadership, are truly appreciated for what they bring to the table, and will have the opportunity to grow and develop their career path in the organization is a surefire method of engaging employees.

(continued)

(*continued*)
Key Takeaways for Individuals

- Does your team leader create an environment that fosters trust, confidence, knowledge that you are a valued member of the team, and your career growth and development?
- Your leader has an incredible impact on these engagement drivers, but it's up to you, too. Don't just stew over an area that frustrates you. Pick one or two areas of focus and answer the questions in a productive manner. Share your suggestions for improvement with your leader in a conversation or some other format.

Key Takeaways for Managers

- Remember the three Cs that inspire trust and confidence: competence, caring, and commitment.
- Over half of employees around the world don't feel valued. Publicly recognize extraordinary achievement and effort and remember that the personal touch (e.g., handwritten notes, dinners, quality time) shows your appreciation.
- Focus on employee growth and development; think beyond formal training courses and include mentoring and career path planning.

Use the Kenexa Focused Listening Questions to uncover areas in which you can do better.

Chapter Bonus Material

Video: Involvement by Dr. Jeffrey Jolton

You have special access to material only available to readers of this book. Watch this exclusive speech by Dr. Jeffrey Jolton as he lays out the secrets to driving worker involvement, how to handle managers who may feel threatened, and how involvement was a key factor in turning around a manufacturing client.

1. Go to www.WeTheBook.com
2. Click the "Bonus Material" button/link
3. Click the link that says "Involvement"
4. Enter the password "confidence" (without the quotation marks)

Enjoy your bonus material!

More Ways to
Drive Engagement

You sort of smell it, don't you, that engagement of people as people. What goes on in meetings, how people talk to each other. You get the sense of energy, engagement, commitment, belief in what the organisation stands for.

—Lord Currie[1]

Growth, recognition, and trust are the three drivers on which managers should stay focused, but there are several other factors that have a significant impact on engagement. Depending on the individual organization, the industry, the country, and even the statistical method used, these other drivers frequently show up in employee surveys:

- Teamwork
- Communication
- Future vision
- Corporate responsibility
- Product/service quality

While nothing can replace a professionally designed and administered employee engagement survey to discover what drivers need to be addressed, what follows will reveal sample questions that can be used in team meetings or with individual employees to help you to get a sense of current engagement levels.

Teamwork

Sudha is a medical illustrator who works on a team that develops health education programs. Other team members include medical writers, Web developers, video producers, and a project manager, to whom she reports. She loves the work she does and is very motivated by the company's mission to improve lives through better health, but she is constantly frustrated by the lack of teamwork. Too often, the project manager just dumps a list of needed illustrations on her desk, along with the technical specs, and the due dates.

Don't they realize she can do more than draw? Maybe if they held a project kickoff meeting and she knew more about the client and goals of the project she could actually help brainstorm impactful images with the writers? Maybe she could remind them of existing art images that could be reused, thus improving product quality without impacting cost. Maybe if she met with the Web designers she could match the artistic style of the overall program. Oh well, time to work on "Image #4: Heart showing thickening in wall lining."

Creating a group effort or fostering teamwork typically refers to how coworkers or organizational units work together to successfully accomplish the goals of the organization. In most cases, high-quality products and services are not the result of the efforts of only one person. Instead, there's an interdependence of many individuals who contribute a variety of skills, areas of expertise, and experience. When these efforts are combined, the products and services offered by an organization are made possible.

Survey Items that Measure Teamwork

The types of survey statements used to measure teamwork include:

1. Employees are encouraged to participate in making decisions that affect their work.
2. My ideas and suggestions count.
3. I feel that I am part of a team.

Teaming is also beneficial to the individual members, typically driving high levels of engagement. Leaders who excel in this area take actions that lead to feelings of inclusion and involvement.

If you suspect that your direct reports are not feeling that they are part of your team, or feel that they don't have enough involvement, use the following Kenexa Focused Listening Questions to guide your dialogue with them.

1. What types of decisions are made that affect your work, to which you don't have the opportunity to give input?
2. What is the best way to solicit your ideas and suggestions?
3. What could be done to improve teamwork in your area?

Don't just ask these questions in order, robotically and passively. Make sure to listen actively and facilitate an open dialogue. Rather than defending your teamwork track record and pointing out all the things you do to drive teamwork, your goal is to uncover what teamwork looks like to them.

Let the answers to the Kenexa Focused Listening Questions guide your actions as a leader. Some generic ideas for how you can increase your team members' feelings of inclusion and teaming include:

1. Research shows that participation in decisions results in greater "buy in" and support of the decision. When changes are being considered that will affect your employees, allow the employees to constructively raise their concerns and/or questions regarding the changes. Allow for as much participation in the decision-making process as the situation warrants. When employees are invited to participate in the decision-making process, they are more likely to support changes that affect them.

2. Allow sufficient time in team meetings to hear from all your direct reports. Encourage participation from the quiet members. Listen for the total message and try to view the speaker's thoughts and ideas from his or her perspective. Use open-ended probes, such as "Tell me more about that" to make certain you understand the other person's point of view fully.

3. Conduct 20- to 30-minute weekly huddles with your immediate team or workgroup. The agenda involves each employee responding to a couple of questions like: What good news do you have, both personal and professional? What customer or team feedback do you have for the group? This could be followed by a report on the progress and discussion of a previously designated topic.

To foster a true sense of teamwork, you need to operate according to your direct reports' notions of inclusion, not your own. You might think you're teaming well because there is little office drama and you all go out for happy hour every Friday night. But their definition may be different. Have open, honest, and specific dialogue about what drives their feelings of belonging. And make sure you have the conversation with your entire team.

Communication

While some would describe Leon as a salesperson for high-end phones, his clients think of him as their consultant for one of their most important customer service systems. Leon loves his clients, but he can't say the same about his employer. In fact it's his loyalty to his customers—many of whom have become his friends—that keeps him in the company.

Communication has always been poor in his company but it's getting worse by the month. The funny thing is that the executives in his company think they're doing a great job communicating. After all, they have the monthly employee newsletter, the company Intranet, the CEO does a video broadcast each quarter, and of course, their weekly metrics memo. But that's all one-way communication. What Leon and his colleagues want is open, two-way communication. He wants to share his ideas for the upcoming tradeshow and know that somebody will consider them. He wants to know about the delay in the new product release, and also be part of the team that crafts the client communication. Why do people in the home office seem to think they have all the answers?

In today's hypercompetitive global economy, companies race to provide everything faster, cheaper, and better. As we all get busier and more externally focused, we, as leaders, can easily forget how critical communication is within a company. Staff meetings, e-mails, and flash reports are just the beginning. These kinds of communication are necessary but not enough. To truly engage employees, you need to also listen and act on what you hear. Use the following questions to foster open, two-way communication, which is key to keeping the team engaged.

Survey Items that Measure Communication

The types of survey statements that are used to measure open, two-way communication include:

1. In this company there is open, honest, two-way communication.
2. The information I need in doing my job is readily available to me.
3. Sufficient effort is made to understand the thoughts and opinions of people who work at my company.

If employee feedback suggests that they are unhappy with regard to lack of adequate communication in the company or within their team or from leaders, you need to try and get to the heart of the problem—is communication really lacking, or is it perhaps the listening part of communication that needs improvement? Discuss the issue with your team members using the Kenexa Focused Learning Questions.

1. What are the specific communication issues that we should be dealing with in a more open manner?
2. What information do you need to be effective in your job and from whom do you need the information?
3. How will additional information make you more effective?

Needless to say, communicate well when discussing communication. Don't ask these questions just for the sake of asking. If you ask but don't act, you'll be in worse trouble down the road than you are now. Let your team members guide you in your actions, but also consider the following generic ideas.

1. Create an open door policy. Let your employees know that they are always welcome to approach you with questions, comments, and concerns. Commit to always answering honestly and without judgment or defensiveness.
2. Conduct a needs analysis to identify the specific information that each employee needs to effectively do his or her job. Based on your findings, determine the most efficient and effective way to communicate the required information.
3. Develop the habit of active listening. Listen with the intent of understanding your employees and not just reacting to what they are saying. Let people know you understand them by paraphrasing the main points that they share with you.

Use the following behaviors when speaking with others: (1) Direct your attention to the speaker and avoid taking phone calls or sifting through mail; (2) Listen for the total message and try to view the speaker's thoughts and ideas from his or her perspective; and (3) Paraphrase what the speaker has said to ensure your understanding of the total message.

Do You Transmit or Transceive?

A radio transmitter sends information in one direction toward the recipient. A transceiver is a device that both transmits and receives signals. When you communicate do you transmit or transceive? In other words, when you transceive, you are transmitting with full knowledge of the listener's frame of reference and mind, and how he will receive what you are saying. This entails talking with, rather than at a person, and is more a meeting of minds and exchange of thoughts on the same plane. Otherwise, both sides will always be transmitting and may or may not connect. In other words, if you do not transceive, you are not on the same wavelength as your listener. If you transceive with an understanding of the recipient, you are effectively increasing engagement, as the other person will sense your insight and will respond positively.

Ultimately, transceiving rather than transmitting can help you expand your sphere of influence and make an impact, whether you are a leader or an employee. You will be combining excellent communication skills with a finely tuned intuition about the situation and your recipient's frame of reference.

Future Vision

Jane is a programmer with a large IT services company. Although she, like all other employees, is a crucial cog in the company's machinery, she is unclear about how exactly her work impacts the larger picture. In fact, she's not even very sure she knows what the larger picture is! Once a quarter, their CEO addresses the entire company and talks about the company's achievements or recent acquisition of another company or the opening of a new office. However, he doesn't really talk about how any of these events are going to affect the company at large, nor does Jane understand how she can help the company achieve its larger objectives.

Contrast this with Jack, who has a clear understanding, thanks to his manager's efforts, of exactly how his work impacts the bottom line and knows his line of sight in terms of the company's future goals. Who do you think is the more engaged of the two? Jane, who is just working at each software programming project she is assigned without realizing its overall importance, or Jack, who knows precisely how he is contributing to the company?

People gain a sense of meaning at work from both achieving excellence in the work itself, and from being part of a greater cause. For one to understand her contribution, therefore, she must know what the long-term vision is for the organization and how she is contributing to it on a daily basis. Others have full frameworks on how to develop a future vision. Our contribution is how to ensure the effective *communication* of the vision.

Survey Items that Measure Future Vision

The types of statement that are used to measure future vision include:

1. Senior management gives employees a clear picture of the direction the company is headed.

2. Senior management demonstrates that employees are important to the success of the company.
3. The leadership of my company has communicated a vision of the future that motivates me.

If you suspect that your direct reports are not aligned to the company vision, or feel that they don't have enough involvement, use the following Kenexa Focused Listening Questions to guide your dialogue with them.

1. In your own words, how would you describe our company's direction and vision?
2. How does senior management demonstrate that employees are important to the success of our company?
3. How well do our senior leaders communicate its vision of the future? What could they do better?

Having a vision poster in the break room wall may serve as a good reminder for all, but it's the responsibility of senior leaders and frontline managers to make sure that employees understand it, see progress toward it, and know how their daily actions are contributing. Try some of the following methods to ensure that they are kept aware of new developments in this area.

1. Review your organization's business direction and goals with your employees at least every quarter. Identify the specific areas where the company is meeting and/or exceeding the goals and where there are opportunities for improvement. Celebrate the achievements and develop strategies for improvement where appropriate.

2. Schedule regular one-on-ones with each employee for the purpose of providing feedback on the employees' strengths and opportunities for growth. Take this opportunity to clarify the link between the employee's work and your organization's objectives. When providing feedback, use specific examples of employees' behaviors.
3. Using the Focused Listening Questions as a basis, initiate a discussion with your employees about their understanding of your organization's strategy and vision and how it is related to their team's success. If their understanding is limited or incorrect, take the necessary steps to help your employees become better informed.

When an employee understands the direction in which the company is headed and also how their work can directly influence the achievement of this vision, they will be inspired to think up new ways in which they can have an impact on helping the company successfully accomplish its long-term objectives.

Corporate Responsibility

Aldo is a recent college graduate and a new employee at one of the world's largest makers of soup. For Aldo and his friends, sustainability isn't a political issue; they don't have a radical agenda, and they believe in a company's right to make a fair profit. Aldo just believes that we need to do right by the planet, and for each other.

He was pleasantly surprised to see so much focus and communication on the company's efforts to be a responsible corporate citizen. His company was making considerable progress toward its stated goals to reduce energy and water consumption, to increase both donated food and volunteer hours of employees, and even to increase the percentage of women holding leadership positions within the company.

Studies from the Kenexa Research Institute reveal that in recent years, an organization's participation in corporate responsibility and environmentally friendly business practices has had a significant influence on both employee engagement and business outcomes. The research shows that employees who view corporate responsibility efforts as positive experience greater pride, satisfaction, and are more likely to recommend their company as a place to work. And employees with favorable opinions of their organization's corporate responsibility activities are more likely to state an intention to stay.

Sustainability is our generation's core issue.
— Mark Parker, CEO, Nike

Survey Items that Measure Corporate Responsibility

The types of survey statements that are used to measure corporate responsibility include:

1. My company does a good job of contributing to the communities in which we live and work.
2. My company's commitment to social responsibility (e.g., community support, protecting the environment, etc.) is genuine.
3. My organization makes business choices that support the environment, such as recycling, energy conservation, and vendor selection.

If you feel your direct reports would benefit from knowing more about the company's corporate responsibility initiatives, use some of the following Kenexa Focused Listening Questions to keep them updated and also to get valuable feedback on what they think about these initiatives.

1. How does our company demonstrate its commitment to the environment?
2. Are there examples of our corporate citizenship that have made you proud that you're part of the organization?
3. How has your role (or lack thereof) in these efforts impacted your attitude toward your job and the organization?

If the answers to these questions give you the impression that the employees need more information on company initiatives, or are interested in participating in them, or feel the company is not doing enough, you can use the following action steps to get them more involved.

1. Assess your employees' awareness of your organization's commitment to being environmentally responsible. Evaluate if your organization needs additional channels to spread its message of environmental responsibility (e.g., intranet, newsletter, e-mail, bulletin board in break room).
2. Using the Focused Listening Questions as a basis, initiate a discussion with your employees about how your organization could respond more appropriately to address the impact of its business activities on the environment.
3. Generate a discussion with your employees about your organization's efforts to be an environmentally responsible

company. Ask your employees how environmentally responsible the company is from their perspective, and how you can collectively improve in meeting this commitment. Take note of any novel suggestions and route them to the appropriate organizational personnel.

For today's organizations, corporate social responsibility is no longer just a good business practice; it reaps many benefits, not least of which are employee engagement and retention and customer appreciation.

Product/Service Quality

There is an often-told quality legend about the great Renaissance artist Michelangelo. He spent four years painting the ceiling of the Sistine Chapel, which when finished included 300 figures depicting nine scenes from the book of Genesis. One day, as Michelangelo lay on his back atop the scaffolds with a small brush in his hand, someone shouted up to him. "Michelangelo, why do you spend so much time on the detail? We can't even see it from down here!" Without hesitation, Michelangelo replied, "Ahh, but God can see it!"

For any business, the quality of the product or service it provides is paramount; employees know intuitively that quality is an antecedent of customer satisfaction. Similar to the satisfaction-service mirror we explored earlier in the book, product/service quality goes both ways. Disengaged workers are likely to deliver lower quality, which will lead to lower customer satisfaction. On the other hand, high quality instills pride in workers, which will raise their engagement levels.

Survey Items that Measure Product/Service Quality

The types of statements that are used to measure product/service quality include:

1. Overall, customers are very satisfied with the products and services they receive from my company.
2. Where I work, we are continually improving the quality of our products and services.
3. Day-to-day decisions demonstrate that quality and improvement are top priorities.
4. Where I work, we set clear performance standards for product/service quality.
5. Leadership is committed to providing high-quality products and services to external customers.

If you know your direct reports are employed in jobs where the company's dedication to customer service and excellent product quality may not be immediately apparent to them, you can use the following Kenexa Focused Listening Questions to gauge the extent of their knowledge, and to facilitate a discussion.

1. How committed do you think senior management is to providing high-quality products and services?
2. What changes have you seen our company make in the past six months to improve the quality of your products and services?
3. What are the obstacles to providing top-quality products and services?
4. Are you clear about the performance standards for which you are accountable?
5. What would it take to raise the overall level of quality here?

Let the answers to the Kenexa Focused Listening Questions guide your actions as a leader. Some generic ideas for how you can increase your team members' knowledge, commitment to quality, and responsiveness to customers include:

1. Ensure you have a formal and ongoing system in place to measure customer satisfaction (e.g., survey, polling). Report on your employees' examples of feedback from happy customers and from those who were disappointed with a product or service encounter. Encourage your employees to take personal responsibility for customers' satisfaction.
2. During a staff meeting, ask your employees what "Quality and Execution" means to them. Identify two or three practical things that the group could do to improve in this area.
3. Determine any issues that might prevent employees from providing optimal service to customers and assign an action team to help address those issues. Identify any communication problems between employees and customers.
4. Identify the goals that compete for quality (e.g., high productivity requirements). Maintain high quality standards while recommending changes that threaten these standards.
5. Develop specific quality goals for each member of the department. Review the goals that you and the department would like to complete and the specific action steps needed to accomplish each goal. Allocate time and resources for each of the steps. Monitor and reward progress.

When processes are in place to ensure and recognize extreme service to customers and consistently first-rate product quality, employees are willing to give their best. They take great pride in their work and in their company, and this shows in their willingness to go the extra mile for a customer, as well in their levels of engagement.

Chapter Summary

Additional Drivers of Engagement

(You can download this summary as a one-page PDF at www
.WeTheBook.com)

The "big three" drivers of employee engagement are
Growth, Recognition, and Trust, which appear as critical
variables in almost all cases studied. Additionally, depending on the company, industry, or even country, our research
shows that six additional factors routinely come up as drivers of engagement:

1. Teamwork (a feeling of involvement and belonging)
2. Communication (a feeling that there is frequent, open
   dialogue)
3. Future Vision (a feeling of inspiration)
4. Corporate Responsibility (a feeling that the employer is a
   good world citizen)
5. Product/Service Quality (a feeling of pride in work)

Key Takeaways for Individuals

- Does your team leader create an environment that fosters
  these six factors?
- Your leader has an incredible impact on these engagement drivers, but it's up to you, too. Don't just stew over
  an area that frustrates you. Pick one or two areas of focus
  and answer the questions in a productive manner. Share
  your suggestions for improvement with your leader in a
  conversation or some other format.

Key Takeaways for Managers

- Nothing is as effective as a professionally designed and administered employee engagement survey, but if you don't have survey data to learn from, you can still talk with your team and individual members about their current feelings concerning these five drivers.

Use the Kenexa Focused Listening Questions to guide your discussions, with the goal of uncovering what actions you can take as a leader to improve engagement.

Epilogue

In January of 2010, The Conference Board released a report revealing that only 45 percent of workers in the United States were satisfied with their jobs, which is the lowest level in the 23-year history of the poll. This dissatisfaction is seen across all ages, income levels, and job types. Despite the presence of the Great Recession, their analysis concludes that the decline of job satisfaction is neither cyclical nor correlated to the economy. The downward trend has been steady and steep, representing a 26 percent drop in satisfaction since 1987.[1]

This is both a social crisis and a business crisis. Emotions at work, whether positive or negative, spill over to the home and cross over to our spouse, children, and friends. Disengagement is harmful to our physical and mental health. For companies, an engaged workforce leads to higher growth and profits and the difference between an engaged and disengaged workforce can have a dramatic impact in total shareholder value.

People view work as either a *job* with a focus on money, a *career* with a focus on advancement, or a *calling* with a focus on contribution. We have an innate tendency to exert our knowledge, skills, and talents in ways that increase our self-esteem, self-worth, and happiness. But when our work is viewed as just a job for a paycheck, we cheat ourselves. When we have goals but they consist of stepping stones to career achievement, our engagement goes up, but it's tenuous and shallow. Only when we pursue the Career-Life Bull's-Eye—the overlap of Passion, Purpose, and Pay—will we find our true calling and maximize our engagement.

However, meaning comes from within and from those with whom we interact. A surgeon may be aware of the value of a difficult, life-saving operation, but its meaning is enhanced when a peer asks permission to scrub-in and observe the procedure, as well as when the patient's son thanks the surgeon for saving his father's life. A teacher knows inherently that his work educating children is meaningful and important, but that meaning is made greater by a parent's thank-you note or positive words from the principal. The source of meaning comes from two sources: (1) internal and (2) external.

The external factors, the culture or environment in which we work, is most shaped by our immediate managers, or leaders. What universally drives engagement are leaders who foster growth and development, recognition and appreciation, and trust and confidence. Less universal but also prevalent are the engagement factors of teamwork, communication, future vision, corporate responsibility, and quality.

The downward trend in satisfaction must be reversed, but it can neither be accomplished by individual nor organization alone. Synergy occurs when the worker and the employer come together in pursuit of engagement. The effect is magnified when the purpose and passion of the individual aligns with the core and BHAG of the organization, when the employee is purposeful about their development and the employer is invested in their growth. The *We* mind-set recognizes that is a shared responsibility with mutual benefits.

When we encounter someone who is disengaged at work we are saddened not over the loss of a single soul, but by the loss of greater potential, the loss to a team, and the impact it has on the individual's family. And when we encounter workers completely engaged in their jobs, and when we hear the infectious enthusiasm in their voices, we are filled with joy knowing their sense of happiness and the impact they are having on those around them.

Your kids, your spouse, your friends, your colleagues—all of us—*we* need you to find meaning and to be engaged at work. *We* need you to be committed to the engagement and alignment of the workers on your team. *We* need each other to reach our shared goals. *We* need to harmonize our lives and our work.

We.

Acknowledgments

The conclusions in this book were informed by survey responses from millions of workers around the world in different jobs, industries, and economies. We thank them for their time and their candor; collectively, their answers have led to insights that benefit all of us who strive to live and work in harmony.

We thank our clients who agreed to share their stories including Aetna, A.P. Moller-Maersk, Kennametal, and Regeneron.

Thanks to the 2,000 Kenexa team members for striving daily to help our clients put the best individual into every job and to create work environments that lead to harmonization.

Special thanks to Shubha Rao Benipuri and Bruce Kneuer for their research, editing, and writing. Thanks to Vernon Bryce, Tony Coe, Jim Donoho, Bill Erickson, Richard Harding, Anne Herman, Jeffrey Jolton, Gavin Kerr, Brenda Kowske, Matt McKelvey, Dave Millner, Peter Timmerman, Sara Weiner, Andrea Watkins, and Jack Wiley for their ideas and words. Thanks to Deb Lee Toth, Mary Lafferty, and Eric Lochner for great illustrations and marketing support.

To Nyla Karsan, who read early, embarrassingly rough drafts and provided both encouragement and ideas that quickly made this book better—thank you.

We also want to acknowledge Matt Holt and Shannon Vargo at John Wiley & Sons, Inc. for seeing in our proposal more than we knew was there.

About Kenexa

Kenexa® helps organizations multiply business success by identifying the best individuals for every job and fostering optimal work environments for every organization. For more than 20 years, Kenexa has studied human behavior and team dynamics in the workplace, and has developed the software solutions, business processes, and expert consulting that help organizations impact positive business outcomes through HR. Kenexa is the only company that offers a comprehensive suite of unified products and services that support the entire employee lifecycle from pre-hire to exit.

Our Integrated Talent Management solutions have impacted the lives of more than 150 million people—this is not based on luck or good fortune, but on intrinsic values hinged upon a mission bigger than ourselves. We seek to transform the global workforce by identifying the best individuals for every job and creating the best work environments for every organization. Our unified products and services include:

- Recruitment Process Outsourcing
- Employment Branding

- Employee Assessments
- Recruitment Technology
- Onboarding
- Performance Management
- Employee Surveys
- Learning Management
- Leadership Solutions

We are proud that:

- We are a market leader in R&D spend—investing $40 million in 2010.
- We have more than 150 million candidates in our recruitment technology systems.
- We assess more than 18 million employees annually.
- We survey more than 10 million employees annually.
- We place more than 52,000 employees through recruitment process outsourcing annually.

For more information about Kenexa solutions, please visit us online at www.Kenexa.com.

How to Reach Us

If you would like more information about Kenexa solutions, make sure to visit www.Kenexa.com. You can also contact us if you are interested in:

- **Employee Engagement Surveys**: Measure how engaged your workforce is and use it as a baseline to grow further engagement.
- **Employee Engagement Training**: Invest in the growth and development of your front-line managers and senior executives and maximize their leadership effectiveness.
- **Speeches and Presentations:** Rudy and Kevin are available to keynote your conference or speak at your next meeting.

If you want to connect with Rudy or Kevin, visit www.Kenexa .com or www.KevinKruse.com. You can also follow us on Twitter at @Kruse and @Kenexa.

Notes

Chapter One: The Return of the Work-Life Blend

1. Heath, Travis. "The Highest Paid Player in the NBA?" *HOOPSWORLD*. Fantasy Sports Ventures, 27 Mar. 2009. Web. 30 May 2010.
2. Abosch, Ken. "What's Next? Projecting the Future of Variable Pay." *Hewitt Presentations from 2009 WorldatWork Conference*. Hewitt. Web. 30 May 2010.
3. Ibid.
4. Gupta, Anil K. "Origin of Agriculture and Domestication of Plants and Animals Linked to Early Holocene Climate Amelioration." *Current Science* 10th ser. 87.1 (2004). Print.
5. "Job." *Merriam-Webster Online*. Web. 30 May 2010.
6. Adams, Carol, Paula Bartley, Judy Lown, and Cathy Loxton. *Under Control: Life in a Nineteenth-Century Silk Factory*. Cambridge: Cambridge University Press, 1983. Print.
7. Meyer, Peter B., and Anastasiya M. Osborne. *Proposed Category System for 1960–2000 Census Occupations*. Washington, DC: U.S. Dept. of Labor, Bureau of Labor Statistics, Office of Productivity and Technology, 2005. Print.
8. "Samuel J. Palmisano." *Corporate Executives & Directors Search Directory*. Forbes. Web. 30 May 2010.

9. "Zachary W. Carter." *Corporate Executives & Directors Search Directory.* Forbes. Web. 30 May 2010.

10. Freedman, Jonah. "SI.com—The Fortunate 50." *SI.com.* Time Inc., Web. 30 May 2010.

11. "CPS Tables." U.S. Bureau of Labor Statistics. Web. 30 May 2010.

12. Stinson, John F. "New Data on Multiple Jobholding Available from the CPS." *Monthly Labor Review,* 1 Mar. 1997. Print.

13. Hildebrand, Deborah S. "Does the 40-Hour Work Week Need Overhauling?: Here's to Working Efficiently in Only 20 Hours a Week." *Suite101.com.* Suite101.com Media Inc., 15 Aug. 2008. Web. 30 May 2010.

14. "Social Security Online History Pages." *Social Security Online—The Official Website of the U.S. Social Security Administration. Social Security Administration.* Web. 30 May 2010.

15. "Historical Background and Development of Social Security." *Social Security Online—The Official Website of the U.S. Social Security Administration.* Social Security Administration. Web. 30 May 2010.

16. "Life Expectancy by Age, 1850–2004." *Infoplease.* Pearson Education, Inc. Web. 30 May 2010.

17. Pear, Robert. "Recession Drains Social Security and Medicare." *New York Times,* 12 May 2009. The New York Times. Web. 30 May 2010.

18. "Pension." Answers.com. Answers Corporation. Web. 30 May 2010.

19. *Mental Health: A Report by the Surgeon General.* Washington, DC: U.S. Department of Health and Human Services, 1999. Web. 30 May 2010.

20. Blue, Laura. "Antidepressant Use Soars." Wellness—A Healthy Balance of the Mind, Body and Spirit. *TIME.com.* Time Inc., 3 Aug. 2009. Web. 30 May 2010.

Chapter Two: Profits Drop When Your Spouse Kicks the Dog

1. Thoits, Peggy A. "Identity Structures and Psychological Well-Being: Gender and Marital Status Comparisons." *Social Psychology Quarterly* 55.3 (1992): 236–256. Print.

2. Matthews, Lisa, Rand Konger, and K.A.S. Wickrama. "Work-Family Conflict and Marital Quality: Mediating Processes." *Social Psychology Quarterly* 59.1 (1996): 62–79. Print.

3. Roberts, Nicole, and Robert Levenson. "The Remains of the Workday: Impact of Job Stress and Exhaustion on Marital Interaction in Police Couples." *Journal of Marriage and the Family* 63.4 (2004): 1052–1067. Print.

4. Hughes, Diane, Ellen Galinsky, and Anne Morris. "The Effects of Job Characteristics on Marital Quality: Specifying Linking Mechanisms." *Journal of Marriage and the Family* 51.1 (1992): 31–42. Print.

5. MacEwen, Karyl, and Julian Barling. "Effects of Maternal Employment Experiences on Children's Behavior via Mood, Cognitive Difficulties, and Parenting Behavior." *Journal of Marriage and the Family* 53.1 (1991): 635–644. Print.

6. Stewart, Wendy, and Julian Barling. "Father's Work Experiences Effect Children's Behaviors via Job-Related Affect and Parenting Behaviors." *Journal of Organizational Behavior* 17.3 (1996): 221–232. Print.

7. Nyberg A., L. Alfredsson, T. Theorell, H. Westerlund, J. Vahtera, and M. Kivimäki. "Managerial Leadership and Ischaemic Heart Disease Among Employees: The Swedish WOLF Study." *Journal of Occupational and Environmental Medicine* 66(1) (2009): 51–55. Print.

8. Kivimaki, Mika, Paivi Leino-Arjas, Ritva Luukkonen, Hilkka Riihimaki, Jussi Vahtera, and Juhani Kirjonen. "Work Stress and Risk of Cardiovascular Mortality: Prospective Cohort Study of Industrial Employees." *BMJ* 325 (2002): 857–860. Print.

9. Tait, Marianne, Margaret Padgett, and Timothy Baldwin. "Job and Life Satisfaction: A Reevaluation of the Strength of the Relationship and Gender Effects as a Function of the Date of the Study." *Journal of Applied Psychology* 74.3 (1989): 502–507. Print.

10. Judge, Timothy, and Shinichiro Watanabe. "Another Look at the Job Satisfaction-Life Satisfaction Relationship." *Journal of Applied Psychology* 78.6 (1993): 939–948. Print.

Chapter Three: Aiming for the Career-Life Bull's-Eye

1. Collins, Jim, and Jerry Porras. *Built to Last.* New York: HarperBusiness, 2004. Print.

2. Collins, Jim, and Jerry Porras. "Building Your Company's Vision." *Harvard Business Review*, 1 Sept. 1996. Print.
3. Kowske, Brenda. "Does Money Motivate?" *Evolve* 2 (2) (2008): 22–24. Print.
4. Easterlin, Richard. "Does Economic Growth Improve the Human Lot?" *Nations and Households in Economic Growth: Essays in Honor of Moses Abramovitz*. New York: Academic, 1974. Print.

Chapter Four: Your Kind of People

1. "Finding the Right Fit—May 23, 2007." News Releases. *OfficeTeam*, 23 May 2007. Web. 30 May 2010.
2. Mills, Elinor. "Meet Google's Culture Czar—Software—Insight." ZDNet Australia—Where Technology Means Business. CBS *Interactive*. 30 Apr. 2007. Web. 30 May 2010.
3. "Internet Shoe Shop's Unique Step—Zappos.com: Revolutionizing How Business Gets Done—with Fun." *Nightline*, ABC News. ABC. 8 July 2008. Television.
4. Fisher, Brenna. "Tony Hsieh: 2009 SUCCESS Achiever of the Year | SUCCESS Magazine | What Achievers Read." SUCCESS Magazine—What Achievers Read. On Newsstands Now! *Success Magazine*. Web. 30 May 2010.

Chapter Five: Do What Companies Do

1. "Education Pays . . ." U.S. Bureau of Labor Statistics. U.S. Department of Labor, 27 May 2010. Web. 30 May 2010.

Chapter Six: Harmonization = Engagement + Alignment

1. Kenexa Research Institute. *WorkTrends® Annual Report 2008*. Kenexa, Inc. Wayne, PA. Print.
2. Wiley, Jack. "Driving Success Through Performance Excellence and Employee Engagement: A 2009 Kenexa Research Institute WorkTrends Report." White Paper. 2009. Print.

3. Sun, Uking. "Special Coverage: China Population." *China Daily*, 13 July 2010. China Daily. Web. 14 July 2010.

Chapter Seven: Engagement Leads to "Better Earnings and Fatter Margins"

1. Welch, Jack, and Suzy Welch. "How Healthy Is Your Company?" *BusinessWeek*. Bloomberg, 8 May 2006. Web. 30 May 2010.
2. Hinkin, Timothy, and J. Bruce Tracey. "The Cost of Turnover: Putting a Price on the Learning Curve." *Cornell Hotel and Restaurant Quarterly* 41.3 (2000): 14–21. Print.
3. Jones, Cheryl. "The Costs of Nursing Turnover, Part 2: Application of the Nursing Turnover Cost Calculation Methodology." *Journal of Nursing Administration* 35.1 (2005) 41–49. Print.
4. Hillmer, Steven, Barbara Hillmer, and Gale McRoberts. "The Real Cost of Turnover: Lessons from a Call Center." *Human Resource Planning* 27 (2004): 34. Print.
5. Hurdy, Craig, Debra Osborn, Anne Herman, and Jeffrey Saltzman. "Solid Investments in Engagement Yield Shareholder Return: The Aetna Story." Kenexa White Paper. 2009. Print.

Chapter Eight: GReAT Managers Focus on <u>G</u>rowth, <u>R</u>ecognition, <u>A</u>nd <u>T</u>rust

1. Saltzman, Jeffrey. "New School Employee Loyalty." Kenexa White Paper. 2009. Print.
2. Wiley, Jack. "Engaging the Employee: A Kenexa® Research Institute WorkTrends® Report." White Paper. 2008. Print.

Chapter Nine: More Ways to Drive Engagement

1. *United Kingdom MacLeod Report*. "Engaging for Success: Enhancing Performance through Employee Engagement." Web. July 2009.

Epilogue

1. Gibbons, John. "I Can't Get No . . . Job Satisfaction, That Is." The Conference Board—Trusted Insights for Business Worldwide. The Conference Board, Jan. 2010. Web. 30 May 2010.
2. Collins, Jim. *Good to Great*. New York: Harper Collins, 2001. Print.
3. Collins, Jim. "The Story of Starbucks Journey to Finding BHAG." Jim Collins. Web. 30 May 2010. <http://www.jimcollins.com/media_topics/all.html>.

Index